WALL to WALL

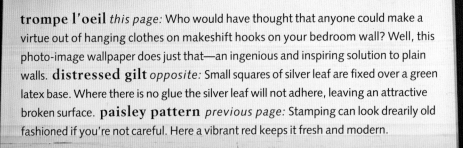

trompe l'oeil *this page:* Who would have thought that anyone could make a virtue out of hanging clothes on makeshift hooks on your bedroom wall? Well, this photo-image wallpaper does just that—an ingenious and inspiring solution to plain walls. **distressed gilt** *opposite:* Small squares of silver leaf are fixed over a green latex base. Where there is no glue the silver leaf will not adhere, leaving an attractive broken surface. **paisley pattern** *previous page:* Stamping can look drearily old fashioned if you're not careful. Here a vibrant red keeps it fresh and modern.

LINDA BARKER

WALL to WALL

100 GREAT TREATMENTS FOR VERTICAL SURFACES

PHOTOGRAPHY BY LUCINDA SYMONS

Clarkson Potter / Publishers
New York

For Lou and Brian
Without you there would have been a lot less fun,
and a lot more words

Published in the United States by Clarkson Potter/Publishers, an imprint of the
Crown Publishing Group, a division of Random House, Inc., New York.
www.crownpublishing.com
www.clarksonpotter.com

Originally published in Great Britain by Jacqui Small, an imprint of
Aurum Press Ltd., in 2005.

Library of Congress Cataloging-in-Publication Data is available upon request.

ISBN 0-307-23652-8

Printed in China

10 9 8 7 6 5 4 3 2 1

First American Edition

CONTENTS

INTRODUCTION

At the risk of stating the obvious, your walls define your house. They hold it up. They hold out the world, and they protect the private places you can go to escape from it. Not only do they carve through the air, emphatically delineating the various rooms in which you live, they also serve as the primary canvasses for any decorating scheme you employ to make that house your home.

Now, you say the word "walls" to some people and they immediately think "things to keep you in" —when I hear the word, I think the very opposite. For me, walls are the first thing I consider when I'm trying to conjure up a room which will ultimately transport its occupants somewhere else— somewhere relaxing, somewhere stimulating, somewhere vibrant, somewhere their heads would love to be even if their bodies can't be bothered to leave the sofa! I'm never happier than when standing in the middle of a bare space, with nothing but the structural shape and the natural light to work with. Eventually, that space will have an activity to host (be it sleeping, eating, bathing, working, entertaining, or just relaxing) and it's my job to enable the room to perform at its very best. Clearly, that doesn't just mean the physical layout and furnishings; just as important is the atmosphere and ambiance a decoration scheme creates. In pursuit of that, the vertical surfaces are always priority number one. Do they need to be decorated in such a way that it will make the room look taller? Do they need to help the sunlight move around the space? Do they need to make a first impression, or would the room be better served if they made a discrete withdrawal? Do they need to shout "I'm over here, I'm over here, pay me some attention!," or do they need to whisper "Put your feet up and relax"? Do they need to help you concentrate, or should they be entertainment in themselves? Do they need to make the occupants feel thrilled, or chilled—or just happy to be home?

THE THRILL OF DESIGNING

I lost count of how many different walls I have decorated, but one thing is absolutely certain, I've never done the same thing twice. Every building has its own character, every room has its own mood, and every wall within that room has its own unique part to play in the final effect. In this book I've put together 100 different ideas for wall treatments. It sounds like a lot, but if they asked me to do the book again, I'd have 100 more. Once you get down to the actual work of decorating with color, texture, and beautiful materials, I'm delighted to say the options are infinite.

As much for convenience as anything else, I've split this book into seven different sections, each collating treatments which use similar materials or a similar approach. However, I must point out that when I design a room it is very rare that I would ever use the same effect on all four walls. Successful schemes are all about balance, but you don't have to balance all the same techniques. Many of the

rooms in this book feature wall treatments which might seem very bold and imposing at first glance, but always remember that by and large you are looking at just one wall of a complete, coordinated decoration scheme. In most cases, the chances are that the rest of the room is finished in more subtle tones, allowing the feature wall technique to do its job properly—to capture and stimulate the eye, without overpowering the senses.

TAKING INSPIRATION

I can honestly say that it has been an absolute pleasure to create all the different room schemes in this book, and I hope you will use it in the way I imagined you would as I was working on it—as a sumptuous menu of methods and materials, from which you can combine just the right ingredients to decorate and rejuvenate the rooms in your own home. I truly hope you enjoy leafing through these pages for information and inspiration, but I don't want any of you to feel you must copy each and every one of the particular projects word for word, color by color. Of course all of these ideas will work well "off the shelf," but I'm sure some will prove to be just a springboard for individual interior schemes of your own. As far as I'm concerned, if you finally close this book and walk away with the stimulation to try something new, the determination to actually start some decorating, and the confidence to express how you really feel in a space you really love, then my work here is done!

natural cover *above left:* Natural textures are paramount to my design work, and I am always looking for new and innovative ways of bringing organic materials into the home. As a lifelong fan of natural flooring, I was excited to learn that this material is equally suitable for paneling walls. Contact adhesive should be used to secure the heavy material in place, and narrow wooden beading will keep the edges neat. **decoupage** *above right:* These stylized peacock motifs were cut from sheets of patterned wrapping paper, and spray adhesive was used to fix them to the wall. A border of peacocks makes a defining edge on plain-colored walls. **vintage wallpaper** *right:* This stunning design was conceived by Australian artist Florence Broadhurst. Here interior guru and stylist Marian Cotterill has used panels of the paper to line the walls of her grand staircase at her home in London.

THE GROUNDWORK

So okay, you have your basic architecture and your lighting done—perhaps you've knocked through some rooms to create great open spaces. Then the first thing you look at in an empty room is the walls. They are the first step in the decorating process—they cover such a huge expanse that they form a critical mass in any space. They dictate the mood of a room in an instant hit and they can say whatever you want them to say—if you want vibrant green walls, you can have them, and they will be the first thing anyone sees when walking in. They will demand to be looked at.

But such huge potential can be scary. Much information is available these days on television and in magazines, but people are still unsure of the way forward, of taking those initial steps. The biggest single area of color or pattern in a room is that of the wall treatment—it is the thing on which everything else hinges. And it is critical to understand this volume in proportion to the other elements in the room. When you start from scratch, it can be almost impossible to imagine what the finished result will be. But there are techniques that I, like other designers, use. And they can help you, too.

VISUAL AIDS

A mood board at its simplest can be no more than a collection of bits of paper with patterns and colors you like, but it is an invaluable decorating tool. It's very easy to get things wrong when you are decorating. You choose a paint color, apply it to the walls, don't like the results, and then lose confidence in your ability to make the right choice. It's easy at this stage to give in and to reach for the white paint, adding to the acres of wall space covered in this non-challenging hue.

An empty room is daunting, so do the groundwork first, to help you keep a firm hold of the idea of the final look you want to create. Collect as much visual reference as you can in the form of samples and swatches and then play around with them. Put colors and patterns next to each other to see how they work. If you find it hard to make the visual jump from a flat collection of samples to imagining the finished room, make a scaled-down three-dimensional model. This can be as basic as a shoe box decorated in your proposed colors and finishes. I sometimes have models made for clients, and the great thing about them is that they give an immediate impression of the proportions of colors and finishes within a space. You will see straight away how dominant the walls are, and you will be able to judge much better whether the treatment you're considering is truly working or whether it is in too much danger of overwhelming the other design elements you've chosen for the room.

You could also use one of the many interior design computer software packages you can now buy. Getting the exact color match can be tricky on a home computer, but what a computer image will show you is how your choices work in three dimensions, which can be an invaluable aid. Anything that

stops you from getting scared about making the final decision is a useful exercise. Before you get anything actually on the wall, do the figuring before it gets expensive and disheartening to rectify. Even I can still get jittery about some of my decorating decisions. Sometimes when I've specified some very bold paint colors for an exhibition house I'm working on, for example, I get last-minute nerves about whether I've made the right choices. But I know when I've done my homework I'm less likely to get it wrong.

EXPLORING COLOR

It's too glib to say people wear the same colors as they would choose for their homes—I have a fabulous orange cardigan in my wardrobe, but it's not a color I would want on my walls. But I have found that people usually have a natural leaning towards a certain color palette. I usually avoid yellow, for example. I find it a very difficult color to work with—it can become too green or turns a nauseous shade in certain lights. Most people have certain colors they feel comfortable with, or inspired by, while others are just a turn-off. This is just the first instinctive phase of color selection, of refining your choices until you come down to the two or three shades in a room that you absolutely love, and that work brilliantly together.

Another of the stages along this route is to physically apply a sample of the color on the walls, and this is where tester pots come in. But don't be tempted to paint two or

vintage wallpaper *above:* Vintage wallpaper has found iconic status in today's interior, and this wonderful original 1960s bamboo pattern is no exception. A set of authentic Tulip chairs and a molded plastic table by the cult Finnish designer Eero Saarinen set an appropriate note for the furnishings, while the retro-style sunburst mirror frame is the perfect finishing touch on the wall.

pebble tiling *right:* This innovative wall covering is much easier to apply than first appears. The pebbles are stuck onto easy-to-handle mesh panels that use regular tile adhesive rather like more familiar mosaic tile panels. A variety of natural finishes are available for this appealingly tactile wall treatment, from inky black pebbles that have a really dramatic effect on a room to these creamy white ones, ideal for a contemporary bathroom or kitchen backsplash.

three small squares in different places around the room. Instead use the whole pot to paint as big a piece of paper as the tester pot will allow (use the back of a scrap of wallpaper, which will be strong enough to take the paint without buckling). Tack that piece of paper to the wall with masking tape so you can judge it in differing light conditions over the course of a couple of days. Then move it somewhere else in the room, perhaps next to some upholstered furniture such as the sofa or the curtains and see how you feel about the color there. Having a bigger expanse of color will give you a much better idea than peering at a tiny patch and trying to decide whether you really like it.

And this holds true for whatever material or application you're considering. Always ask for the biggest sample you can get, or if necessary buy a single roll of wallpaper, a half yard of fabric, the smallest size paint can, or a few tiles in the line you like. This might seem rather indulgent, but a little financial outlay at this stage can save you from making a very expensive mistake later.

LIGHT AND TEXTURE

When designing and decorating your walls, it is very easy to get swept up in the practical aspects of the process and forget to step back occasionally and appreciate the effect of interior design's most vital ingredient—light. Without light, after all, all your hard work is for nothing. But ignoring the direction and quality of light that will fall on your walls can be almost as bad. However, if you plan ahead for the effects of that illumination, the results can be truly stunning.

Light loves texture. Flat colors can look radiant in the right light, but there is nothing like the tactile, three-dimensional qualities that tone, texture, shadow, and highlights will bring to a wall. The first thing you need to do when planning a textured wall effect is to define the type of light that will fall on the finished result. Is it mostly flat-lit from a window on the opposite side of the room? Is it mainly side-lit from a window on an adjoining wall? What happens to that wall at night? Does artificial light tumble down from a ceiling fixture, or is the light splashed from wall sconces or a nearby table lamp? The more side-lit your wall, the greater the effect of any textured finish. You could cover an entire wall with egg cartons, but if it was only ever lit from directly in front you would never see any of the tell-tale shadows that can make a textured wall so striking.

Light aside, the other defining factor and appealing feature of a textured wall is, of course, touch. A three-dimensional wall finish can be just as much a treat for the fingertips as it is for the eye. Ribbed wallpapers, natural wood grain, stippled plaster, cork, stone, metal leaf—be bold in your choices and don't be afraid to cover large areas with some of these dramatic materials. However, the golden rule is, always try a little bit of your chosen effect on the wall for a few days before you commit to the whole thing—just to make sure the light loves it as much as you do.

EXPLORING THE POSSIBILITIES

Familiarize yourself with all the amazing products that are available. Go to all the consumer shows you can. Saturate yourself with what's new. There is nothing like actually touching and feeling a product to really appreciate it, and fairs are the ideal place to do that—it's what they are set up for. Talk to the sales people—they will be flattered by your interest, and most good salespeople have a genuine interest in what they are selling that they want to impart to you. They are great providers of the information that is important to your decision-making process. If you are interested in a more unusual wall finish, visit specialized suppliers, and again, talk to the people there. Ask about their product and

what you can do with it, how it is applied. See if they have any photographs of what other people have done to help inspire you. It is this shared enthusiasm and excitement that can spark off ideas.

Go to the designer showrooms for a more interesting take on decorating than you would get in a chain store. Small places like this might only carry ten rolls of wallpaper and a limited range of paints and fabrics, but what they have will be carefully considered, so some of the decisions have already been made for you through their own filtering process. The people who run these places are immersed in the world of interior design and have the time to spend helping you make your choices.

THE THRILL OF CREATING

The most important thing to remember when you have a decorating project is that the planning is a lovely process in itself, so enjoy it as much as you intend to enjoy the finished result. It's like getting ready for a party—it can often be the best bit. Don't be too rigid in your ideas: allow yourself to be drawn to a vibrant color or a startling pattern, and then explore how you feel about it. The fun of the decorating process is allowing yourself to be inspired—by a show-stopping wallpaper design, by a gorgeous piece of mahogany veneer, by some sparkly crystals. Designing can make your heart race and keep you awake at night. Don't be scared—embrace that thrill of conveying your idea into reality.

photo montage *above left:* This photo of the Trevi fountain in Rome was snapped on my last vacation. Displaying your best shots on the wall beats putting them in an album where no one gets to see them. You could have a different image for each canvas, but splitting a single image makes a strong impact. Several print companies offer this service. **fabric curtain** *above right:* In a featureless room a wall of curtaining makes for an interesting wall treatment. Lightweight voiles will have the added benefit of moving slightly as people sweep past. Fabric is stapled to a wood strip at ceiling height and the staples disguised with a strip of narrow beading. **graphic edge** *right:* A wall-edge detail of repeated paisley stamps is given a modern feel by partnering it with big, bold painted geometric panels in linking colors.

P
A
I
N
T

glitter
bold colors
colorwash
antiquing
graduated
barcode
stripes
stamping
stencils
overhead projector
mural
fresco
freehand details

glitter *this page:* Paint companies are becoming increasingly clever in their quest to bring exciting new products to their customers. These glitter particles are suspended in a clear gel solution that is simply painted over a chosen base color. Once dry, any traces of the clear gel are gone and the glitter pieces are bonded to the wall. Layers of glitter can be built up to create a denser glitter wall.

monochromatic *this page:*
A monochromatic wall treatment can be just as vibrant and exciting as the boldest color palette. Here a muted palette of soft grays range from the most delicate of shades to a steely graphite gray. The small variations between the colors are achieved by simply adding increasing amounts of white paint to a good, basic gray. The trick to the knife-edge precision of the color blocks is a straight-edged carpenter's level, low-tack masking tape, and lots of patience.

P A I N T

As an interior designer, I am staggered by what you can achieve with a few paint colors and simple brushes. Flat walls can be transformed from bland, uninspiring, empty planes to fabulous surfaces that almost pulsate with vibrant color. Different finishes can create anything from a delicately soft texture that brings warmth and comfort to a glowing expanse of metallic paint that will bounce back sunlight with an almost magical shimmer. Paint is a master of disguise. Do you want that surprisingly covetable effect of age and the buildup of years of subtle patination? My antiquing effect (see page 19) will give you just that. Do you want a specific motif or design, or the painterly effect of your very own mural? Take a look at the ideas in this chapter and it will be the paint can you reach for every time.

You can use paint in blocks and bands of contrasting color and texture to completely change the perceived shape of a room, to give the impression of increased volume or more elegant proportions. Horizontal stripes, like those on a T-shirt, will widen the surface; in fashion terms this is not always a good thing, but for a small or awkwardly shaped room, a little visual trickery like this can be extremely beneficial. Vertical stripes in a low-ceilinged room will have a lengthening effect, again a fantastic device for those of us with vertically challenged rooms.

In order to achieve a contemporary look for your home, you may want to partner your free-form paint effects with a neatly tailored flat paint color on some of the walls within a room. The last thing you want to be reminded of is the paint effect craze of the 1980s when the decorating *cognoscente* were a little obsessed with the overuse of sponged, stippled, and rag-rolled paint finishes obliterating nearly every surface.

Picking the color or colors for paint effects can be a daunting task. There are thousands to choose from, with the paint giants providing the lion's share of the market, but with the smaller producers also offering a select choice of colors. It's difficult to know where to start, and research shows that many of us will reach for the can of cream paint before any other. Ah! cream—this

Of all the wall treatments there are, paint is inevitably the one that is most familiar to us— who among us does not have a painted wall somewhere in our home? But we shouldn't let its ubiquity blind us to the dazzling variety of effects that can be created with a few humble cans of **PAINT**. Using clever and versatile techniques, you can create marvelous finishes—from boldly graphic stripes to elegantly meandering murals—that can transform the look and feel of a room with luminous color and superbly tactile texture.

perfectly acceptable shade of off-white has now become a synonym for "boring" and there are millions of homes out there decorated with it that are testament to this. But in our quest for lightness and brightness in our homes, it's hardly surprising that sales of white and cream paint have always preceded cans of color.

But we should be braver. Color is the first thing that strikes you when walking into a room. It has vibrancy and impact, and demands to be looked at. It is also, particularly in paint terms, the easiest thing to apply to the walls and probably the cheapest. You would think then it's easy, but of all the component parts that go into making a successful room scheme, paint color is the most difficult to get right. Back to the rule book then to give us a steer in the right direction. The color wheel provides us with the strongest clues about how to get color right. Based on the three primary colors—red, yellow, and blue—spaced evenly all around the wheel, secondary colors are those that develop between the merging primaries. Further on still are the tertiary colors, which are those that merge between the secondaries. From this simple color wheel then, certain observations can be made.

Cool colors, such as those containing blue and green, are called receding colors, whereas on the opposite side of the wheel we have the reds and oranges or advancing colors, which are warm. Cool, receding colors are best employed to produce an airy feel to a space, whereas warm, advancing colors will seemingly close down and cozy up the available space and make it feel more welcoming. A narrow room can be made to appear wider with the use of cool receding colors, while a long corridor can be made to appear shorter with a warm color painted on the end wall.

colorwash *opposite:* In its simplest form, a colorwash effect is vibrant and energetic. A dynamic finish for uneven walls and smooth freshly plastered walls alike, the color swirls like a piece of modern art. **graduated color** *below:* This delicate paint finish is achieved using a gradual diffusing of color. Bands of yellow paint are applied over a pale cream base coat and a wide brush is used to tease the color into the blank central space. A glaze is added to the yellow to allow for an extended play of the paint. This means the paints tend to stay wet and workable for longer, allowing you to move the paint around until the graduation is even. This is a fabulous finish and would look great in both modern and traditional homes, although I would avoid bumpy uneven walls; they just don't do the effect justice.

dark color *left:* Sometimes an absence of color can be the most dramatic statement to make. Rich, dark tones suck in the light and can produce powerful areas of visual punctuation in an otherwise more conventional room scheme. It's also a great way to frame and display favorite accessories.

bold colors *opposite:* This vibrant red would be almost impossible to bear were it not for the balance of its complement, which allows the eye to rest. Too much red can induce over-activity, which is why it is used in some fast-food chains, where they want customers to eat quickly and move along. In the right quantities, though, it can be energizing, perfect in this kitchen where it is framed by a less imposing color.

complementary colors

Colors opposite each other on the color wheel are called complementary. Using a little of a color's complement can prevent it from becoming overbearing. Impressionist painters used this principal; avoiding black altogether, they used a color's complement to darken or create shade. If a color I've chosen is too vibrant, I try to add a little of its complement to the can. The complementary color knocks out the vibrancy of a garish shade to lessen the ferocity and make an altogether more palatable dulled-down shade.

opposite: There are lots of ways to achieve an antiqued wall finish, but this is probably the easiest I know. Colors are crucial to the overall look; here I have applied a solid base coat of a metallic silver latex, over which I have scrubbed a scant layer of dark gray/blue. Aim to destroy the bristles of your decorating brush to get the perfect look. Build up the color in those places that naturally accumulate most wear, such as in corners and around switches.

1 The base color is integral to the overall look of the paint finish. On this occasion I used a pale teal blue color underneath my washed layer. Of course, bolder colors can be used to create some dramatic finishes, but remember to exercise some caution—the '80s had their moment a good while back. Let down the top-coat color—off-white latex in this case—with enough water to produce a light cream consistency. Scrub the thinned paint over the dried base to build up a cloudy layer of color. Avoid any obvious pattern making at all costs by continuously working the paint and varying the brush strokes.

left: The rigorous brushing and scrubbing technique produces a fragile cloudy appearance that is ideally suited to this pretty hall and stairway.

1

cloudy colorwash

This colorwash has a much softer and more refined finish than the colorwash shown on page 14, which illustrates just how versatile this paint finish can be. I love the delicacy and translucency of the paint, which takes on an almost watery appearance. In this version, the darker-colored layer is applied as a base color, so the effect is a complete reversal of the previous colorwash, in which I used a much stronger top color. The pale thinned top color allows the base color to dapple through for a gentle finish that is very calming.

graduated paint

A less refined graduation than that shown on page 15, this has a more lively and energetic impact. There are no glazes mixed with the graduating paint color, so the effect is less exacting and so is easy to execute. Suitable colors are those in the mid tones, such as denim blue and dusky lilac—like the color I have used here. Pastel pinks and baby blues would also be lovely, but avoid anything too pale or too dark. For the latter I would suggest the more precise and tailored glazed graduation. Your base coat should be fairly neutral—white or cream are usually the most suitable.

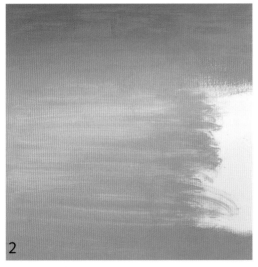

1 Divide your chosen graduating color into three by decanting two measures into two paint buckets. To the first paint bucket add half the amount again of white paint. To the second paint bucket add an equal amount of white. With the original strength paint, this will give you three graduating colors. Start with the darkest color at the top of the wall and paint a wide band of paint across the wall. Working quickly, paint the second mid-tone color across the center of the wall in the same way.

2 Using a damp, wide brush, start to graduate these two colors together, merging the darker paint into the mid-tone color and blending the two colors so that you lose the effect of the painted bands. Then paint the palest color at baseboard level and continue as before with a wet brush, merging the pale and mid-tone colors together to achieve a seamless flow of graduated color from ceiling to floor.

opposite: This is a great finish for a casual, almost hippy home because it is quite romantic and bohemian. It forms a perfect backdrop for the current vintage look.

striping the color

Barcodes and stripes can be employed in every room, and almost any combination of colors can used, depending on the final effect you are looking for. The success of this look lies in the neat, tailored precision of the stripes. Not only visually stunning as a feature wall or as an all-over wall effect, barcodes also allow the designer to play spatial games within the room. Stripes and barcodes can be as restrained and sophisticated as they can be wild and crazy; the important thing is to create a scheme to suit your space.

blue-striped bedroom
left: These bold stripes work perfectly on the bedhead wall of this bedroom. The graphic linearity is echoed in the clean angular lines of the furniture, and the stripes are also picked up on the bedding.

wide stripes *opposite:* These stripes are refreshingly up to date because of the use of both matte and metallic paint colors. Part of their success too, lies in the choice of color. Deeply dramatic and seductive, this rich olive green is complemented exquisitely by the gun-metal gray metallic latex. The knife-edge is achieved with low-tack masking tape and good brushwork. Paint the metallic stripes over the flat base coat, never the other way around. Use a loaded paintbrush and brush over the tape toward the center of each stripe; never towards the tape, which could force paint under the tape, resulting in an uneven edge.

thick and thin

The key to success with this all-over feature wall lies with the careful selection of paint colors. It's rare that I err on the side of caution, but in this case I suggest you make your selection of colors from a paint chart, then group these together on a piece of cardboard, making a kind of mood board. Move the colors around for a couple of days, adding or subtracting ones until you are certain the color balance is one you can live with.

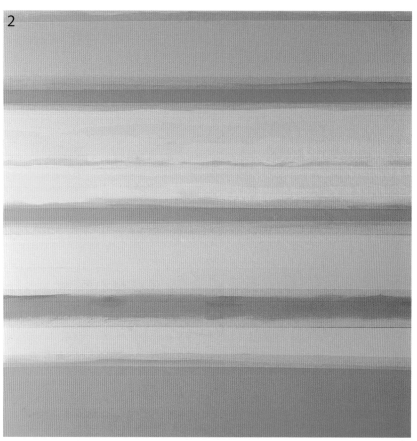

1 The base color is important as this will form some of the barcodes; use the color you would like to see most prominent in your room as the base. A carpenter's level is the best way of keeping any horizontal lines accurate. Mark the lines with pencil. The number and thickness of lines is largely up to you. I tend to work by eye for these finishes, adding more stripes or gauging the ratio of thick versus thin depending on the look I'm after.

2 Use low-tack masking tape to create your neat crisp edges. Mask off as many stripes as you can in one session. Some stripes will be so small the tape will obscure them initially, but they can be added on a second round of painting.

3 Start to pull the tape off carefully. Then, if there are further stripes to add, do so only when the first barcodes stripes are thoroughly dry.

opposite: Lots of stripes can be headache-inducing in a small space. But they look fantastic where their scale can be appreciated, such as in a hallway.

living color *below:* The soft natural tones of this barcode design are combined with baby blue, tonally very similar to the naturals and therefore restful on the eye, a gentle effect until the inclusion of a deep chocolatey eggplant, which adds a frisson to the whole look, creating a very vibrant effect.

half and half *opposite:* Sometimes just a little detail is all that is required to add a little dynamic to walls. Here I have sectioned off an upper part of a wall to add crisp, modern barcode stripes. Plenty of the white wall color is allowed to show through to keep the effect fresh and balanced. If these gaps were filled in, the overall effect would be too top-heavy and dominant. The barcodes lend themselves beautifully to living rooms, but the neat precision of the stripes could enhance a sleek modern bedroom.

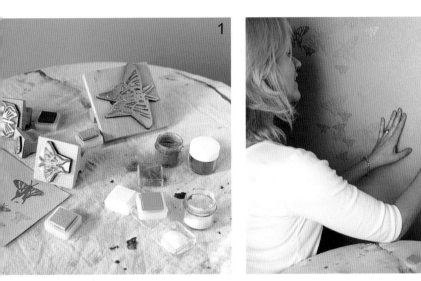

butterfly stamps

Butterflies are enjoying a revival at the moment, thanks in part to fashion designers like Matthew Williamson, whose beautifully printed textiles are adorned with delicate butterflies and feathers. We owe our thanks to the red-carpet parades then, as the interior designers are never far behind the *fashionistas*. Tonally the colors I've chosen here are close, creating a gentle pattern, but imagine a pale pink wall with black butterflies or perhaps a purple glitter butterfly on a purple wall.

1 I used four butterfly stamps of different sizes and varying designs to increase the naturalistic effect. Try out your colors on a piece of cardboard first to see how they work together before applying them to the wall.

2 Remember that the empty space on the wall between the butterflies is as important as the patterned areas; keep an eye on the developing pattern by standing back from your work and continually assessing the emerging design to maintain a free-flowing feel.

3 To add a little luminescence to the occasional motif, I applied sparkly glitter dust over the paint surface of some of the butterflies. You need to do this while the paint is still wet, holding a piece of paper underneath as you work to catch any glitter that does not stick.

opposite: A random pattern of butterflies is perfect for a delicate wall frieze—the effect should be like a rising cloud of diaphanous wings fluttering against the sky.

contemporary stencils

In a book about innovative wall treatments, some people may be surprised to discover more than a passing nod to traditional stenciling. However, far from being tired and boring, I think you will find that the stenciling patterns I've included on these pages and the next are not only dynamic but have strong potential for even the most modern homes. When pattern and color are powerfully of the moment, these beautifully designed images from the Stencil Library have enormous relevance.

flower power

The essential part of this wall treatment is getting the stencil right—the design is everything. An over-fussy shape would soon become wearing repeated all over the walls. Well, my choice of color wasn't too bad either! Once the effect was complete, I thought it would be striking to position a few darker floral motifs over the others to bring a slight change to the uniformed regularity. I just like to stir it up a little!

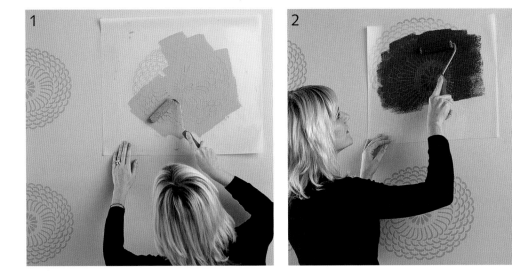

1 This stencil forms a regular grid pattern over the whole wall. Create the grid in one of two ways: either measure the wall using a retractable tape and plot in vertical and horizontal lines using a carpenter's level; or, more simply, use the shape of the stencil sheet. Use repositioning spray to hold the stencil in place. Apply the first color with a small paint roller.

2 Reposition the stencil systematically over the wall to build up the overall pattern. Select which patterns will feature the second stencil overlay, and place the second stencil over them. Make a note of the position if you want to repeat it exactly elsewhere, although I chose a random effect for this wall.

3 Carefully pull away the stencil in order to reveal the finished pattern. This combination of colors is one of my favorites and brings a certain dynamic to a regular repeat wall pattern.

opposite: This is as simple as it gets, a regular stencil over a plain wall; but it looks as good as expensive hand-blocked wallpaper.

peacock stencil

Stenciling has had plenty of bad press over the years, and admittedly some of it is justified, but one look at these oversized peacock stencils and I think I can earn back your respect. I decorated my feathers with a combination of paint colors and textures; a little metallic sparkle on the feathery fronds adds a touch of glamour. For other effects you should simply experiment: using gloss varnish rather than paint would produce a subtle but incredibly striking feather say, on a deep, richly painted wall.

1 Place the stencil onto the wall surface using a little repositioning spray. Here you can see the first peacock feather has already been stenciled so the colors are already evident on the stencil. As each feather is a replica of the last, I have used the same colors to build up each feather.

2 Build up the largest color areas first, in this case the fronds and the center of the peacock feather. Use a latex brush or a small foam roller to apply the paint. Each feather is so large that it requires three separate stencils to build one complete motif. Once the first section is painted, lift away the stencil (keep it flat on an old newspaper until you need it again), position the second part of the stencil and repeat until the image is complete.

3 Small darker tips are added to the edges of the feather for a more realistic finish. Do this with a small decorator's brush or artist's brush. As with most stenciled motifs, the image really comes into its own once the stencil sheet is pulled away from the wall, revealing its full beauty at the last moment.

opposite: These dramatic designs are so gorgeous they wouldn't look out of place in a chic loft apartment. Stenciling has been reborn in the twenty-first century!

overhead projector

One of my all-time favorites, this technique never fails to impress, and it really can be as easy as taking a tracing from a book. A simple system of lights and mirrors projects the image onto the wall ready for you to trace around. You need to work in a semi-shaded position in order for the equipment to project the image sharply enough onto the wall for you to trace around. Projectors are easy to rent for a couple of days; check your local phone directory for details, or you may be able to borrow one from your place of work or a local school.

1

1 Set up the projector so the light source and image fill the available space. The image could be a photograph you have taken yourself and then transferred via a photocopy machine onto a sheet of clear transparent film. The projector works in reverse, rather like a mirror, so make sure you are happy with the image this way around; otherwise, flip it over.

Use thinned gray latex paint to trace along the projected lines of the image, standing between the light source and the wall occasionally so you can check the progress of your work. If the feature wall is in a heavy traffic area, you may want to protect the finished work with a coat of non-yellowing acrylic varnish.

opposite: These dramatic pylons by artist Sally Barker are graphically imposing, but rather than being austere like their real counterparts, I like the lacelike effect this photographic image has when projected and then painted onto the wall.

painted mural

A pretty daunting undertaking you may think, but actually, like most things, if you break this dramatic wall treatment down into its component parts, you see how the image is gradually built up into a beautiful picture. I used masses of tester pots for this room—lots of tonal blues, greens, and earth colors create a naturalistic scene. The more confident artist can paint birds or animals to make the mural realistic—see how you go.

1 Choose a source material to refer to as you paint the mural. Don't feel this is cheating; we all need a little guidance. Apply your main colors to the wall in broad patches over a basic wall color. Soften the edges slightly with a dry artist's brush.

2 Apply lighter and darker tones of the same colors using a sea sponge to create a stippled finish that resembles foliage in a forest. Recreate a feeling of leafy density using shadowy and light-splashed areas for a three-dimensional effect.

3 Use a pencil to draw, then paint the tree trunks, branches, and twigs using a delicate artist's brush. Use a dampened sea sponge to introduce delicate foliage over the branches at tree canopy height. Then, with a narrow artist's brush, use long thin downward strokes to create delicate grasses.

opposite: You could use decoupage animals, birds, and butterflies over the mural, but don't use this idea as a short-cut option. The right choice of initial image is integral to the success of the overall look.

updated fresco

Fresco is a very old classical method of wall painting. In the time-honored tradition, natural colored pigments are mixed with water and painted into the surface of plaster while it is still wet. The lime becomes a binding agent for the pigment, and the painting becomes a permanent surface on the wall due to chemical reactions. So successful was this method that many Greek, Etruscan, and Roman murals are still in evidence today.

1 Paint the wall a good strong base color, in this case dark blue, then use several thinned washes of latex to mottle the surface of the flat paint, making it more interesting.

2 Draw on the tree and branch outlines using a pencil and use off-white latex to paint these onto the wall. Mentally decide on a light source for your trees, enabling you to put in realistic light and shadows around the trunks and thicker branches. A small bird was painted into the tree at this stage and a curious snake that curled around the base of the tree; no apple, though!

3 Use a flat artist's brush to paint broad single brushstroke leaves. Knock back or soften the tree foliage while the leaves are still not quite dry to create a dulled fresco effect, using a natural sea sponge and a little blue or brown latex paint.

opposite: This is a method of capturing the look and feel of a fresco with modern easy-to-use paint, rather than slavishly recreating the original technique.

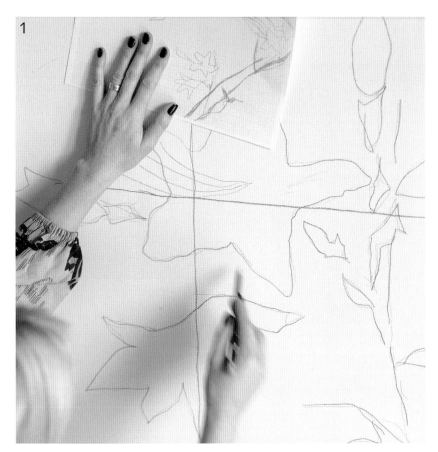

freehand details

The success of this design is due to its scale. A further dynamic is introduced with an offset, painted taupe panel which animates the eye, but anchors the blossom beautifully. The linear style of Japanese floral art is perfect for two-dimensional work—little or no chiaroscuro, an absence of spatial or aerial perspective, and no attempt to develop a natural pattern of light and shade means that emulating the motif directly onto a wall is relatively easy.

1 Make an accurate linear tracing of the blossom and then draw a pencil-line grid over the surface of your tracing. Divide the height of the image into five sections; then create equal divisions across the width of the image.

2 Use a slightly thinned black acrylic paint to color in the twiggy parts of the mural. Allow the edges of your painted line to wobble slightly, as a perfectly neat and precise line will look too clinical and clean cut.

3 Fill in the pale pink parts of the blossom first. Let them dry, adding the darker centers next and the flower stamens last of all. The finished mural can be protected with a layer of clear flat acrylic varnish which should be rollered on after a day or so, allowing the mural to dry completely first.

opposite: Sourcing your image is crucial to the finished look. Choose from a copyright-free book that is easier to copy rather than a piece of china, particularly if this is your first attempt at painting freehand on a grand scale.

APPLICATIONS

distressed gilding
plain gilding
antiqued gilding
detail gilding
gilded letters
pattern gilding
lettering
decals
tattoos
plaster
gesso stencil

distressed gilding *opposite:* Neatness and precision don't always cut it in design: sometimes it can be the downright flaky that hits the right note, and here is a prime example. It's the distressed edges of this silver-leaf gilding that contrast with the smooth sheen of the silver for undeniably good looks.

polished plaster *this page:* Plaster gets a raw deal these days. Most people slap it on, let it dry, and then paint or paper over it. Given a little thought, plaster can play a much more exciting role in your design schemes. Combine it with some pigment, polish it with wax, and you end up with this stunning finish.

A P P L I C A T I O N S

I'm a great believer that there is nothing wrong with having a little fun in your home. It is important to include elements that make you smile, or that give you a small jolt of pleasure when you see them. I love trying out different and new ideas—that is what excites me about being a designer, it's what gives me a buzz. But sometimes the thought of applying a particular treatment over the entire room, or even over one whole wall, can be too scary. What's great about many of these ideas, such as the gilding projects (pages 46 to 53) or the tattoos (pages 56 to 57) is that they can be applied over a manageable area. And the results are fabulous.

Many of these ideas are unashamedly glamorous. They allow you to inject a shot of your own personality into your surroundings, to add accessories to your home as you would to your wardrobe. I operate from the standpoint that the textbook decorating rules are there to be broken—I think it's when you're playing "outside the box" that the most exciting and freshest ideas can emerge. But even I have to admit that there are some physical rules that always hold true, and one of these is that the contrast of textures between a flat finish and a shiny one will never fail to please. So balance your embellishments with a little flat paint elsewhere in the room and you cannot fail.

Though we sometimes hanker after a little bit of glitz, remember, a little of this sort of thing does go a long way. Too much adornment can be wearing to look at and to live with, and you'll soon be reaching for a can of latex to cover up your painstakingly applied creative masterpiece if you overdo it. Go for a single feature wall to make a decorating statement. A hallway can be an ideal location for this type of treatment—it announces to the world from the outset that yours is a house with personality and character, but it is not a room that anyone lingers in, so the effect stays fresh.

One of my all-time favorite wall finishes—and one I have a lot of in my own home—is plaster. It's a fantastic material and so versatile. For a very basic effect it can be left unfinished,

Adding just a little something to your walls is guaranteed to add a great deal to your finished design. In this book, **APPLICATIONS** can be anything from a discreet cluster of pretty butterflies fluttering in a corner to an entire wall of gold gilding, but whatever the technique you choose to employ the intention is always the same—the applications in this section are meant to intrigue, to entertain, and to compellingly draw the eye exactly where you want it as someone first enters the room.

with that unique Pepto-Bismol-pink color that is impossible to reproduce. Plaster can be rollered to look like stone; it can be used to create all sorts of three-dimensional effects. It can be left with an almost crumbly surface that harks back to its humble origins as wattle and daub.

This very versatility means you can use it almost anywhere in the home. Unfinished plaster is breathable, so it releases any water it absorbs from the atmosphere, making it a great choice of wall finish even in damp areas such as bathrooms and kitchens. And if you need to make the most of light, a polished plaster wall is the perfect surface for reflecting any available light. Polishing plaster creates incredibly attractive results. When the particles are rubbed together, the abrasion causes a shine that can be anywhere from a slight sheen to a brilliant gloss. A polished plaster wall is a real thing of beauty, with a delicate luminescence. And the finish is so tactile, so smooth, that it positively invites touch. But it can be waxed to protect that precious effect from all those curious fingers.

Polished plaster has a romantic and noble history in many cultures. Tadelakt, for example, is the wall coating that was traditionally used in the *hammams*, or Turkish baths, of Morocco. Made with Marrakech lime, it produces an incredibly smooth finish that is watertight. "Venetian plaster" is a modern variation of the traditional Italian *marmorino* or *stucco lustro*. It's incredible to think we can have in our homes a finish that has its origins thousands of years ago in grand Italian palazzos. And this venerable art is very much alive today—there are numerous Internet sites offering courses in Morocco and Italy teaching the skills needed to apply these specialized finishes, if that interests you.

tinted plaster *opposite:* Conventional plastering techniques usually give you a perfectly flat finish, but applied with a studied amount of "disregard" even modern plaster will dry with a beautiful textured surface. Adding a subtle tint to a plaster finish will make the overall result even more stunning. **crystal tattoo** *below:* One of the more unusual finishes in this book, but also one of the most ornate, wall tattoos like this are best used sparingly. Repeated across a large expanse of wall they can be intimidating, but used individually or in small groups they provide the perfect finishing touch. Delivered as finished designs held together on backing paper, these particular patterns are from Swarovski.

plain gilding

In its traditional form, gilding is a time-honored profession employing extremely skilled craftspeople who carry out their trade to exacting standards. For the more humble decorator, there are quicker-to-use, more modern materials on hand. Here, an ultra-thin transfer aluminum leaf simulates real silver, and because one side of the leaf is temporarily adhered to the backing paper, it is much easier to handle than the real thing.

1 Apply a quick coat of spray-on adhesive to the shiny side of the transfer leaf, press onto the prepared base color, peel off the backing paper: that's all that is needed for a gilded wall. Repeat this process as necessary to cover the whole wall, or create a panel of silver as I have done here. Draw pencil lines across the panel periodically to keep everything in line.

2 If a large part of your gilded wall is to be obstructed, by a television unit or a bookcase, for example, it makes sense to gild only a panel of the wall. Mark this panel on the wall prior to gilding using a carpenter's level and pencil, and continue as above, using the pencil lines as your guide.

3 Peel away the backing paper and smooth down the leaf with the back of your hand or a soft cloth. Apply adhesive to the next square and repeat. Seal the finished gilded area with a coat of clear acrylic gloss varnish to protect it.

opposite: Fabulous contemporary gilded finishes are a fraction of the cost of real gold or silver leaf, and they are far quicker and easier to apply.

antiqued gilding

Brushing shellac varnish over a newly gilded surface knocks back the brand-new shininess of the surface and adds a rich tonal patination. Here I've antiqued a bronze metal leaf, but it is a process that can be used for any metallic leaf, from pinkish coppers to cool silvers and aluminum. Brush the shellac over the gilded area using a small decorator's brush. Deeper tonal variations can be achieved by applying additional layers of shellac. This finish doesn't require any further protection.

1 The two horizontal stripes I've created here bring a contemporary look to a room and the antique patination is enhanced by the attractive green ocher latex on the walls. Apply the gilding transfer leaf as shown on pages 46 to 47, only this time you are obviously gilding between two pre-determined pencil lines to form the bands. Then apply the shellac over the finished leaf using a small decorator's brush.

2 Work the shellac into the surface of the gilding, and while the surface is still wet, (shellac dries quickly so you need to work fast), scrub the surface using the bristles of the brush to rub away some of the gilding material. This distresses the surface further and enhances the antiqued nature of the effect.

opposite: This method of antiqued gilding may be used over an entire wall surface if required, the effect is largely about what will suit your home and your style of decoration.

detail gilding

Metal leaf can be bought in small booklets of approximately twenty-five leaves, and although it is relatively inexpensive anyway, this method of gilding uses only a small number of leaves; an average room would probably only need two books. The size of the gilded leaf will determine the size of the painted square in which it is placed. Although there is no need for strict mathematical precision when positioning the gilded square, the larger, painted squares need to be very accurate.

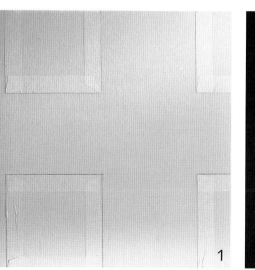

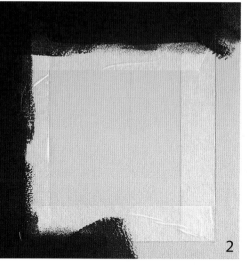

1 Mark the larger painted square on the wall, then position the tape on the inside of the plotted squares. Use a retractable steel measure for accuracy and low-tack masking tape to create a neat crisp edge.

2 Paint the wall your chosen color, applying color up to the taped edge. Two rows of squares like these create an arresting feature wall, but for a whole room you may prefer to have just a single band of squares.

3 Apply a little spray adhesive to the back of the transfer leaf and position it centrally over the painted square. Pull the tape from the wall as soon as the painting is finished—there is no need to wait until it is dry. An application of acrylic gloss varnish will protect the gilded surface from tarnishing with exposure to light.

opposite: For those who prefer an elegant and symmetrical approach to their decorating, this precise style of detail gilding with its contrast between light and dark is just the thing.

pattern gilding

Gilding comes in many forms, but this gilded stencil crayon has to be the easiest way I know of adding a little glitz. A single isolated, gilded pattern within a wall that has an abundance of decoration is a lovely way of catching the eye and adding a bit of sparkle. These deep plum colors are great for creating a look of glamour, particularly in a bedroom where these delicate chrysanthemum patterns and this feeling of opulence can be appreciated. So that a pattern of this intensity doesn't become overwhelming, you can create restful spaces, room for the eye to literally take a break. A good parchment latex on the other walls would balance the darker colors.

1 I stenciled the chrysanthemum blossom in a random fashion all over the painted walls, overlapping the flower designs occasionally to increase the freeform effect. I deliberately kept the stenciled color tonally very similar to the base color, to enhance the effect of the individual gilded flowers. When the paint work was dry, I positioned the same stencil, only this time using a gilded stencil crayon to create a little gilded detail. A single golden flowerhead stenciled every square yard or so is all that is needed.

opposite: Parts of the stenciled chrysanthemums overlap each other to create a more fluid pattern. For lovers of symmetry, however, a simple grid system may be drawn onto the wall first, resulting in a more uniform, regular pattern.

well-read walls

Using lettering in different forms is a delightfully easy way to add interest around your walls. Using Latin script is always intriguing as guests try to decipher your messages, and to read the same instantly recognizable phrase could become tiring. Around my bathroom walls I once had "now wash your hands please" in Latin, which seemed to entertain people rather successfully. The creative word play is up to you: isolated words, well-known phrases, or simpy your own initials all work brilliantly.

printed lettering *left:*
"Home Sweet Home" is as simple a message as it gets, but you must agree it looks so much more stylish in Latin. Computers will obviously do the hard work for you; all you need to do is select the font and the letter size and print out your chosen phrase. Any other way is simply arduous, so find a friendly computer owner if you don't have one. Cut around the letters individually to make them appear professionally written and stick them along a base line drawn on the wall.
gilded letters *opposite:*
These letters are a bit of fun and absolutely adorable. They literally make a statement in a room, and I have used them many times to great effect. Personally I like mixing up the letter sizes and the different gilding colors to create a more eclectic look. Concentrating the lettering on one feature wall will have a greater impact.

DOMUS · DULCIS · DOM

paint tattoos

This is a relatively new concept in walls, and one that I think works exceptionally well. It is based on the same principle as kids' skin tattoos, the sort you see inside bubble gum wrappers and such like. Stick the tattoo over the surface (skin or wall!), apply a damp cloth on the reverse, wait a minute or two, then peel away the backing paper to reveal the tattoo. It was always a bit like magic as a child—now I get to do it on full-blown grown-up walls!

1 This particular wall tattoo is applied to the walls as rectangular strips. Measure the appropriate wall and decide where the wall tattoos should be placed. In this case horizontal stripes were best, but vertical columns or even panels of pattern would work well. Using a carpenter's level and a pencil, draw yourself some guide lines on the wall. Peel off the protective layer of film that covers the tattoo. Place the edge of the paper against your drawn pencil line; the slightly adhesive surface on the tattoo holds the sheet in place. Repeat with each sheet until you have covered the area you want.

2 Use a damp cloth or sponge to dampen the back of the tattoo sheets. All the paper must be moist enough to loosen the tattoo from its backing, but take care not to allow drips to fall and mark your painted walls.

3 After two minutes or so, test the edge of the tattoo, peeling back a corner of the backing paper to check if the design is released. If all is okay, carefully remove the backing paper. Wait a little while longer if necessary.

opposite: Two horizontal stripes make for a visually widening wall treatment, although the pattern could just as easily run vertically for a heightening effect.

textured plaster *left:* This humble material is transformed with the right equipment. Here a specialist plasterer has rolled on a plaster paste to achieve this open texture, and as it dries the highest ridges of plaster are flattened back using a plastic spatula to give the wall finish this characteristic horizontal drag. This is a beautifully practical surface for a bathroom, as steam is absorbed into the porous plaster and then slowly released as the temperature and humidity drops, so no more condensation!

the magic of plaster

A plaster wall has an innate integrity somehow. Whether it be roughcast bare render or an incredibly sophisticated polished finish, it has an inherent beauty and substance that can contribute so much to the look and atmosphere of your home. Isn't it incredible that such basic raw ingredients—at their simplest, dust, water, and a basic binder—can, when mixed together, become something so very sophisticated? Earth and ground rock can be transformed through a process that is almost like alchemy.

waxed plaster *this page:* This most basic material is virtually unrecognizable on this wall. With an incredibly high-luster shine, the surface looks like an expensive lacquer. In the hands of an expert, a basic colored plaster is transformed. An initial layer of plaster is trawled on to a depth of only ⅛ inch. A second layer is then applied over the first using a beveled edge stainless steel trowel. The magic occurs with the friction of one layer of plaster being applied over another, resulting in this highly tactile finish. A final buffing of wax adds another degree of shine to this classy finish.

gesso stencil

Gesso is a delicate liquid made from chalk, traditionally used under gilding in the furniture and picture framing trade. It is incredibly malleable and can be combed or pushed into various shapes or patterns, which then can be decorated or left plain. Here I have pushed a modern acrylic polymer gesso (thickened with a little powder filler) through a cut stencil to achieve a delicate raised branch effect. You can create a similar effect using ordinary modern ready-mixed filler or wood putty.

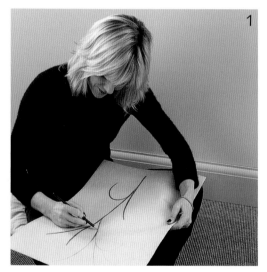

1 Draw the branch shape on a sheet of stencil board. I have sketched mine freehand but you may want to look at a real twig for reference if you need to or copy a design. Thicken up the drawn lines and cut them out using a utility blade. It's worth bearing in mind that any ultra-thin lines will clog up with the gesso. Keep the design clean and spare for the easiest application and the best finished results.

2 Place the stencil against the wall and secure it with tabs of masking tape. Push the thickened gesso or filler through the stencil and then pull away the stencil board before it is dry, taking care not to lift the gesso off the wall. When the gesso has dried, sand any raised pieces if they stand too high, as they can become quite sharp.

opposite: I animated my gesso branches with photocopied decoupage butterflies taken from a copyright-free sourcebook—they flutter around in a random pattern.

W
A
L
L
P
A
P
E
R

photo wall
hand printed
retro vibrant
floral
flocked
mixed patterns
chinoiserie
vintage
positive + negative
textured
metallic
grass cloth
self-paint
picture frames
interactive stickers
masks
decoupage

W A L L P A P E R

Ten years ago the choice of wallpaper in your average decorating shop was just dull. The designs and colors were bland and boring (more stripes, anyone?), and it's not surprising that we rushed past the rows of tired tacky prints straight to the paint shelves to quench our thirst for stimulation and color. But now the *zeitgeist* is definitely with wallpaper and many designers and artists are tapping into it, making it one of the most creative areas of the moment. There's even a fantastic crossover of designers working in other areas, such as Neisha Crosland and Wayne Hemingway. Fashion meets decorating at so many levels—just think how many clothing designers now have home collections to enable you to create a whole lifestyle package. And pattern seems to be everywhere at the moment. When I go clothes shopping with my daughter, I can't help but notice the stores have decked themselves out with big brash in-your-face pattern. I think it is just so exciting.

Of course, all of this is great for us, because it gives us so much more choice about what we can do with our homes. If Boho chic is what makes you happy, go for the full-on glamour of 1950's Hollywood-style wallpaper, or the incomparable elegance of luxurious flock. These glamorous wallpapers unmistakeably hark back to that golden age of interiors. And if you have walls like these, there can be no compromise with the rest of the furniture either—it's elegance and luxury all the way with this look.

If you feel more comfortable with a more restrained environment, check out the selection of natural grass papers (see page 73)—they create muted texture and interest without screaming for attention. What is important is that you are happy in your home, that the choices you make for your walls reflect your personality.

Wallpaper is so versatile—it's very easy to get involved in the pattern-making process. There are some amazing interactive papers that allow you to put your personal stamp on them (see pages 74 to 77). Or you can make your own selection of the beautiful papers and just play with different shapes and scales, a process I love. These smaller projects are ideal if you're a bit

If there is one area of home decorating more than any other that is enjoying a huge renaissance at the moment, it is **WALLPAPER**, and deservedly so in my opinion. The fashion for flat paint that has dominated the decorating market for the last ten years is now well and truly over, and the current vogue is for big, bold patterns. This massive explosion of interest has produced some truly amazing designs, so make your choice from the fantastic papers that are out there to add a new energy and vibrancy to your home.

daunted by the process of wallpapering. The thought of using specialized equipment such as the pasting table and a plumb line and then negotiating a long strip of pasted paper onto the wall can be intimidating, but you can start small and pick up the skills you need as you go.

Along with some amazing output from contemporary artists, designers, and even some photographers, there's been a rediscovery of great wallpapers from the past. The work of key designers from the last century, such as the Australian Florence Broadhurst (see page 70), is now hugely in demand. After being a painter, a dancer, and even running a dress shop for a short while, Florence Broadhurst established her revolutionary wallpaper business during the 1950s. By her death in 1977 her "vigorous designs for modern living"—hundreds of luxurious and unique patterns in vivid shades ranging from fuchsia pink and lime green to rich silvers and golds—were being exported all over the world. Today Florence Broadhurst's designs can be found covering the walls of the hippest and trendiest places in town.

This general resurgence of interest in quality, high-end wallpapers is already having a trickle-down effect on the more mass-market lines. And wallpapers from the cheaper end of the price range can be made really interesting and dynamic too, if you mix them in different ways (see page 68 for some ideas). Even traditional and usually more conservative paper manufacturers are now producing some exuberant patterns that we can use with abandon all around the house—even the kitchen. So don't miss out on the decorating revival of the moment. You like to enjoy the latest fashions in your wardrobe, so doesn't your home deserve the same treatment?

floral *opposite:* This exquisite wallpaper may look very modern, but it is decades old and only now is enjoying a revival. The pattern is just one of many conceived by Australian-born artist and entrepreneur Florence Broadhurst in her creative heydays of the 1930s and '40s. **photo wall** *below:* This image is enlarged to a size selected by you, then stripped into wallpaper drops all carefully numbered for an easy transfer onto the wall. **grass cloth** *previous pages:* In my quest for all things natural, I discovered this beautiful wallpaper composed of horizontal grasses stitched onto a natural-colored backing fabric. **vintage** *previous pages:* It is hard to imagine this room with a simple coat of paint; without pattern or paper it would lose most of its appeal.

an explosion of talent

If you thought wallpaper was what your granny bought when she wanted to revamp her front room, then today's designs will blow your socks off. Young, exciting, and vibrant, the new crop of wallpaper designs are a must have for anyone looking to get the latest vibe. More often than not, the papers are used for feature walls where a dramatic statement is paramount. If you are a little weary of the ubiquitous beige/taupe/cappuccino/latte groove, this could be just the thing your walls have been looking for.

hand-printed paper *left:* Wallpaper is enjoying a revival and hallelujah for that—now at last we can enjoy fabulous pattern and color in our homes. So inspiring is this new trend that new designers fresh out of art school are providing us with some of the most glorious papers ever seen. Louise Body, an up-and-coming young designer, produced this fabulous design.
retro vibrant *opposite:* Older, traditional suppliers are also getting in on the act. Cole & Son, one of the finest paper manufacturers, is providing us with some of the most dramatic papers I've seen for a long time, and this is one of their best.

the changing face of wallpaper

In its fight for commercial survival, wallpaper has actually come full circle. In its early incarnations it was loud, lavish, and luxurious—wonderfully ornate and prohibitively expensive. As it became increasingly mass market, somehow the patterns seemed to shrink and shrink. By the time I was a child, all my parents had to choose from was roll after roll of delicate designs, apparently all in orange or brown. Thankfully, happy days are here again. Wallpaper designs are at their best, and take it from me, bold is back.

mixed patterns *left:* Not everything needs to be bold and bright—lots of homes are too small for vibrant colors and patterns. Neutrals, however, need not necessarily spell boring. Combining similar color tones with different patterns is an excellent way of introducing a fresh and modern look to wallpaper with just the right degree of subtlety.

chinoiserie *opposite:* One of the most desirable of wallpapers, this chinoiserie-style paper by de Gournay is the ultimate in luxury. Handpainted on silk, each panel is unique. To commission an entire room entails plotting out the room. De Gournay then hand-paints the silk panels to fit exactly around your space, taking into account doorways, windows, and so on for a perfect tailored fit.

flocked wallpaper *this page:* A million miles away from the red flock traditionally found in nightclubs, this chic black flocking adds a vibrant bohemian glamour to an upstairs landing. Set within panels on the wall, the wallpaper becomes the picture within the frame, creating a wonderfully graphic positive + negative effect. A room-dividing screen lined with the same flocked wallpaper adds to the opulent feeling created in this small space.
metallic *opposite:* This bedroom, a real Hollywood-style boudoir, has been papered in an incredibly stylish design by 1930s Australian designer Florence Broadhurst. The paper has a silver foil backing, which is why it sparkles so beautifully as it reflects all available light.

modern floral *this page:* Osborne & Little is a well-recognized producer of excellent wallpapers, but this paper to my mind is one of the team's most beautiful. A floral design that is both contemporary and unfussy is a difficult one to get right, but this one does just that. Sleek modern furniture and styling to match place this bedroom firmly in the modern homes category.
grass cloth wallpaper *opposite:* The inherent beauty of this wallcovering lies in the use of natural materials. The fibers that run horizontally across this paper are real pieces of woven grass with their intrinsic and natural beauty and variation in colorings, which gives the paper a unique look that brings a soft and cozy feeling to whichever room it is used in.

self-paint papers

As kids we would have been punished
for expressing any of our creativity
on the walls, but with these papers
it's exactly this sort of activity that is
encouraged—if in their own bedrooms,
I hasten to add. These naive daisy
motifs are absolutely delightful when
seen en masse, floor to ceiling. It's
not just for children's rooms though—
this paper looks surprisingly elegant
in a hallway and would add a certain
quirkiness in a kitchen. The child-like
flowers can look surprisingly
sophisticated if they are teamed
with the right accessories.

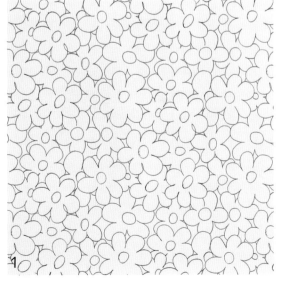

1 This sprawling all-over design is applied to as large an area of the walls as you
wish to cover, matching up the design in the same way you would apply any
other patterned wallpaper. You then have a blank canvas, ready to customize
however you wish. It's like having a giant-size coloring book.

opposite: A soft pink latex is diluted 50:50 with water and the resulting wash used
to paint in occasional, random petals on the daisy motif. The centers of the flowers are
colored lime green, in a sharp contrast to the sugary pink.
above: A blue color wash is liberally brushed over the entire surface. When the wash is dry,
color in the daisy centers with a gold stencil crayon or a spot of gold metallic paint.

picture frames

The ultimate in do-it-yourself wallpaper, this design actually requires you to literally fill in the gaps. For the more artistically challenged, you can always use the frames, as I have done here, as a photograph wall. Kids may be freely encouraged to paint on their walls if this paper is applied to their bedroom walls—all you need to add is a few pencils.

1 Stick the paper to your walls in the normal way. Some or all of the empty frames can then be filled with a painted, drawn, or photo image. It's worth remembering that this paper will look great with or without pictures; with only a few frames filled; or with the whole lot completed. It's all about having fun.

left: Family snapshots can be displayed on the wall rather than hidden away in a photo album.

interactive stickers

This pretty printed paper by designer Rachel Kelly is adorned with elegant footwear. Rachel has successfully forged a name for herself in the design world with her innovative line of so-called interactive papers. Not content with the pretty pattern on its own, each roll of paper comes with a set of rub-down transfer prints, so your own wallpaper is a unique interpretation of your own creativity.

1 The rolls of paper are put on the wall in the good old-fashioned time-honored way. This paper seems to be tailormade for girlie bedrooms, but don't let me limit your imagination. If I were creating a feature wall, I think I would coordinate it with flat-painted pastel pink walls.

2 The stickers are positioned by you, directly over the paper. Hold the transfer sheet over the paper and rub the back of the transfer with the back of a spoon. You will need to press reasonably hard to transfer the sticker. Continue with this application process until all the stickers are used up.

above: Embrace the full-on girlie glamour with lots of pretty cushions piled high. Suspended from the ceiling, a floaty net canopy drapes over the sides of the bed.

wallpaper masks

A brand-new concept for walls, these masks create dramatic statements for any interior. They are particularly effective if applied over existing wallpaper; I love the pattern-on-pattern effect. The acrylic masks are available mail order and, despite their size, are easy to use. Three or four motifs on one wall gives a dramatic eye-catching look, but other effects can be produced by overlapping the patterns slightly.

1 Spray the back of the wall mask with a little repositioning spray. This will hold the mask close against the wall and help prevent paint from seeping through; it will also create a neat crisp edge at the edges of the pattern.

2 Roller paint over the entire wall mask, bearing in mind that you will need to reposition the mask once it has been covered. This Shaker-blue colored latex is a pretty contrast to the pink-patterned wallpaper underneath.

3 Peel away the wall mask and reposition it on another section of the wall. Roller on the paint as before and continue in the same way until you have used the mask often enough to create the dynamic look you're after.

opposite: Think of the natural tones of fresh flowers and plants that inspire you most, and emulate this look by choosing a harmonizing base paint color and wallpaper.

decoupage

Wrapping paper is an area where designers are getting noticed—some patterns are so inspirational that I often buy four or five sheets to use purely as source material for my interior design projects. In particular, these sheets designed by designer Neisha Crosland were simply too good to wrap up and send away. With a diverse collection of different patterns and colors it could be difficult to keep the look cohesive, but with the addition of three bright red chopstick style slashes across the wall, the disks feel perfectly composed.

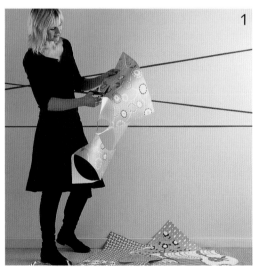

1 Use masking tape as a guide to paint your stripes onto your base coat. You will have to let each stripe dry before applying another over the top. Use a dinner plate as your template for the wrapping paper disks. You can use different sizes if you like, but I chose to keep my circles a uniform size. Cut out as many paper disks as you feel is right for your wall; estimate approximately 5 disks for every linear yard as a rough guide. Sometimes you will use more and sometimes less to create a seemingly random pattern.

2 Play around with the circles, using the painted lines to anchor the overall composition. When you are happy with the placing, use spray adhesive to stick the disks onto the wall. Make sure that the glue coverage goes up to the edges of each disk; otherwise, the disks will start to lift up and become torn or tacky, ruining the clean crisp graphic effect you are striving for.

opposite: Low-tack masking tape was used to create the red lines that dissect the wall.

FABRIC

leather
fabric panels
lined
padded panels
lace laminates
dividing screens
textured
suede

fabric panels *opposite:* On a wall above a stairwell, a sari is hung to great visual effect. By simply threading the fabric on a dowel, held in place with a couple of cup hooks, the bottom of the fabric is left to hang loose, which results in a little wafting movement of the cloth when people move up and down the stairs. **leather** *this page:* Leather is a beautiful fabric to work with and it has lots of applications for the interior designer. From leather tiles for the floor, we now have leather tiles for the walls, which are easy to make yourself if you can get hold of enough leather to cover an entire wall, or there are specialists you can buy from. I stuck the leather to 12-inch-square boards using contact adhesive, then trimmed each one with a blade.

FABRIC

Fabric has always been one of the most important elements in interior decoration. We are all used to swathing our windows with material in the form of curtains and blinds, and can appreciate what a huge impact those choices have on a room. We are quite at home with the idea of sorting through different swatches to make carefully considered decisions about what material to cover the sofa in, what to choose for the scatter cushions, and even what to dress our beds in.

Even with this high degree of familiarity, it can still take a bit of a leap of the imagination to start applying fabric to our walls. But to ignore fabric as a potential wall covering is to discount a whole range of fabulous effects that we cannot achieve with any other type of material or application.

The unique appeal of fabric lies in its yielding quality. Loosely draped around the walls, it is marvelous for cheating the dimensions of a room—softening the edges gives the impression of space beyond because the boundaries are blurred. There are no sharp demarcations so the eye doesn't quite know where the space ends. Fabric can also contain and disguise a multitude of sins—from cracked plasterwork to ugly pipes.

But quite apart from these potential practical benefits, for me, having my walls swathed in fabric is the ultimate in grandeur and luxury. No other wall covering can give us quite the same cocooning effect, and it is this inviting softness that makes it wonderfully suited to bedrooms, where texture is all important. Fabric can also transform a hallway: imagine entering your home through a womblike entrance way swathed in textured velvet or silk. What would be more welcoming than such enveloping richness?

When you're using fabric on your walls, the first decision is the type. Consider the sort of mood you are after—think of the very different effects created by a delicate cotton voile with its chic elegance, and a sumptuous gold-embroidered Indian sari silk, with an intoxicating exuberance that is impossible to ignore. Do you want the

What can be more appealing to the senses—not just your visual sense but the sense of touch—than a room swathed in fabric? Use FABRIC on your walls to surround yourself in wonderfully tactile layers for an incomparable sense of absolute luxury or to create the ultimate comfort zone. You can create a breathtaking bedroom with the brilliance of an expanse of shocking red watered silk, or jazz up a living room by hanging huge panels of a modern geometric print. Fabric has endless applications on your walls.

opulence and exquisite luxury of voluminous folds of diaphanous fabric swathed across an entire wall, which will lift and sway sensually in the breeze to add movement? Or are you after the crisper, more contemporary effect of fabric tightly stretched across strips of wood to show off the detail and energy of a modern geometric print?

There's a really strong tradition of designers who worked in fabric—people like Ray Eames, who worked with her furniture designer husband Charles producing designs such as Crosspatch, or Lucienne Day, wife of British furniture designer Robin Day, whose fabric designs such as Calyx and Sunrise defined the mid-twentieth century. These iconic designs are now just as admired and coveted as the modern art that originally inspired them, and applying them to your walls is a great way to incorporate original art into your home.

Be inspired by what's out there. I'm really excited at the moment by the revival of the funky Italian designers Missoni and Pucci, who produce such fabulous abstract prints. And though you might regard fabric as a traditional material, it's not immune to technology. Recent innovations include metallic fibers woven into the textile, layers of fabrics fused together, and the application of photographic imagery onto cloth—these fresh designs all bring a buzz and energy to your home.

Fabric on walls was commonplace centuries ago in the form of animal skins and tapestries. They were used to indicate status and wealth, as well as supply much-needed insulation in the days before central heating. We can play with this tradition in the twenty-first century and bring it up to date by using more modern counterparts of those ancient textiles. Try butter-soft suede, for example, or distressed leather tiles—perfect in a bathroom because they are breathable.

damask *opposite:* You can play with different fabrics by draping a length over a door for a temporary injection of interest. It's a feature in the meantime, and you can judge the effect of the colors and textures in the room before committing to something more permanent, such as having a fabric panel or lining an entire wall.

woven webbing *below:* This woven webbing strip is usually out of sight underneath chairs and sofas, holding the upholstery together. But I must confess I love the natural rough good looks of this tape and thought it would make a fabulous trimming. Simple weaving techniques make this border gloriously easy to do. Staple the long horizontal strips and weave the smaller verticals between, leaving no gaps. A wooden strip secured at the top and bottom disguises the rough edges.

fabric-lined walls

This striking patterned fabric creates a luxurious bedhead wall combined with paint on the other walls, and a single fabric-lined wall can be no more tricky to put up than a roll or two of wallpaper. The key to success lies in the careful battening of the walls. Once this is in place, it's simply a question of stapling the fabric to the strips of wood and then covering the staples. For entire rooms covered in fabric, I would call in the experts, but it's certainly worth trying it yourself if it's a single wall without too many switches and sockets to negotiate.

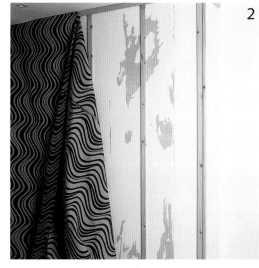

2

1 Batten the wall with regularly spaced narrow wood strips. The vertical battens should correspond to the width of the fabric. Drill holes for anchor plugs then screw the battens in place, using butt joints where they meet. Each light switch socket must be battened, too, as the fabric needs to be cut around these. Use a cable detector to determine where power cables are under the walls, so you do not drill though them, and work with the power turned off to reduce any risk.

2 Each width of fabric is secured to the batten, both at the top and bottom and at the sides of the wall. A good upholsterer can supply strips of thick cardboard, which can be inserted into the long vertical edges of fabric drops as they are stapled onto the wood. This creates a neat crisp edge to the vertical seams which otherwise would pucker against the staples when pulled tight. The stapled edges are disguised under the fabric seams, but those that cannot be hidden should be covered with a length of matching ribbon glued in place over the row of staples.

opposite: The vibrant weave of this fabric could overpower a room if used on all walls. Using it against a bedhead wall is a perfect compromise, bringing a richness of texture and pattern.

padded fabric panels

These boards can be made to any size to fit your space—adapt the measurements to suit your width of fabric to make sure you are getting the best usage from it. Plywood, masonite, or composite boards are all suitable materials to use for the base. You can edge the back of each board with wood for strength, then mount the boards on the wall with mirror brackets.

1 Prepare the boards by cutting them to size or have your lumberyard do it for you. Tack strips of wood all around the edges on the reverse of the boards. You may need to cut your boards according to the shape of the wall you are covering.

2 Cover the top of each of the boards with a piece of batting that has been cut to fit; then place the fabric layer over this. Number each board as you progress. This will correspond to the mounting of each board onto the wall so as to continue any pattern repeat as it occurs.

3 Turn the board over very carefully without disturbing the batting and fabric. Staple the fabric to the back of the board, working from the center of each side out. Create a neat miter fold at each corner, then attach the mirror brackets to the back before positioning the board on the wall.

opposite: The extra layer of batting beneath the fabric gives these panels a soft cushiony spring to the touch for an added dimension of texture and comfort.

lace laminates

This clever design by artist Emma Jeffs actually traps a length of black lace between two layers of plastic. The reverse layer is self adhesive, resulting in a unique type of wall treatment that can be applied as conventional paper is, covering the entire wall, or in panels as I have done here. The starkness of the black lace is contrasted prettily with a soft pastel pink latex base color, which ghosts through the lace pattern in addition to framing each panel of lace.

1 Measure the lace against the wall to determine how many panels you need. It is possible to halve the width of the laminate if you prefer to create narrower panels. Alternatively, you may prefer to choose smaller squares of laminate to display as a grid pattern over your walls.

2 Secure the top edge of the laminate by peeling back a little of the backing paper. As you progress down the wall pull away increasing amounts of the backing paper until you have secured the whole panel. Smooth it down carefully as you go, removing any air bubbles that may have become trapped.

opposite: Lace shakes off its granny image to move out of the country cottage and into the modern home: an old-fashioned fabric is given a brand-new application.

fabric-covered screen

left: Here, a do-it-yourself screen
uses a pretty sprawling damask
fabric on the front and reverse of
a wood panel. The stained strips
of wood cover all the raw edges of
fabric, and the panels are then
hinged together to form a zigzag.

large canvas *opposite:*

Commercially available screens
are becoming ever more popular.
This photographic image spans
four panels, which can stretch
across an open space to effectively
separate two distinct areas.

using dividing screens

Sometimes it is necessary to delineate space, and the easiest way to do this is to have
a portable fabric screen. In a large open-plan space these portable walls are absolutely
necessary for blanking off areas that are less frequently used or simply areas that you don't
want people to see. In smaller rooms, for example a spare bedroom, you may want to
double up the space for a workroom or an office, so the screen becomes invaluable.
An attractive fabric cover adds to the decorative appeal of a room.

textured walls that work

We all know that it is simply not acceptable to cover the sides of the bathtub with a piece of leftover carpet, and common decency prevents us from nailing the shag pile to the bedroom walls, but how do we get coveted texture onto our wall without losing our style credentials? Super textures like our suede fringed walls are an instant hit if used with restraint, whereas less dominating textures like this fake suede is the sort of wall covering that would look great in any room or on any number of walls.

faux suede walls *left:* This suede texture looks like the real thing, but is in fact a very good look-alike—a man-made material bonded onto a thick wallpaper backing. The rich texture is tactile but still hardwearing, so it is perfect for either a luxurious living room or a bedroom. It would look beautiful as a feature wall in contrast to either a flat latex or a super-glossy paint—either extreme is a good look.

real suede fringed rug *opposite:* Unlike its good-looking but fake neighbor, this wall is every bit the real thing. These suede rugs hung on the wall are hugely tactile; perfect for a bedroom. Battening the wall first will make mounting the rugs easy—simply tack the rugs to the strips of wood.

T I L I N G

pebbles *this page:* Progress is a wonderful thing, especially when it saves me time making walls look gorgeous. Just a couple of thousand years ago, it would have taken the might of the Roman Empire to produce intricate mosaic walls like this, and now look—pebbles on a roll. All sorts of natural stone and ceramic products can now be bought as tesselating mesh-backed squares. **slate** *opposite:* There was a time when the conventions of polite society constrained the use of slate to the floor, or the roof. Happily, those days are gone, and slate walls are making an appearance everywhere, from public buildings to private homes. If you shop around, you will find there are many subtle variations of slate tiles available, each with its own signature combination of tone and texture. However, one quality they all share is color, and an expanse of dark-tiled wall is not for the faint hearted. That said, the finished effect is both bold, and pretty much bullet-proof in terms of finish, so my advice is to be brave with your slate and drag it out into the public areas of your home for maximum effect.

TILING

It might sound sad, but my idea of a great day out is one spent at a really good tiling shop. I think they are truly inspirational places, filled with goodies drawn from all around the world, from incredibly delicate Moroccan encaustics to those chunky industrial glass blocks, from handmade tiles that are miniature works of art to chunky slabs of earthy terracotta I just can't resist touching. I'm just like a child in a toyshop, not knowing what exciting thing to look at next.

There's such a wealth of colors, textures, and shapes available, and you can get so much inspiration about how to decorate your walls by exploring what's out there. The tiles themselves may be made from rigid materials, but they throw up endless opportunities for wonderful pattern-making. You can play with texture and shapes, from smooth mirrorlike surfaces to chunky round pebbles, and even create dynamic rhythms with geometric shapes and the endless repetition of hundreds of tiny mosaic squares.

Cleverly used, tiling can be used to alter the perceived shape and proportions of a room. If you have a long narrow room—the shape of many bathrooms—you could tile the far wall only in strongly colored or textured tiles, balancing it with pale colors and flat finishes on the other walls. This will have the effect of foreshortening the room and making it seem wider. Tiles can also be a great distracting device, forming a blanket disguise for potentially ugly additions in a room such as unsightly plumbing, boxed-in pipes or the ducting for extractor hoods. If all surfaces are covered with the same material, disruptions such as these will blend smoothly in with the rest. Use small mosiac tiles if this is the effect you need—they are the most successful size for negotiating awkward corners and turns seamlessy.

Alternatively you can, of course, use tiles to define certain features, to make them stand out rather than recede. The backsplash above a sink or the area around a bathtub are the obvious locations for such displays, combining the merits of protecting the walls from water damage and creating a focal point in one hit. I give some ideas for this on pages 108 and 109.

In addition to being eternally and classically attractive, tiles simply cannot be beaten for their practicality, and when it comes to choosing a wall treatment for a bathroom or a kitchen, of all the alternatives **TILING** wins hands down. Tiles are tough, durable, and waterproof—I can't think of any other material that comes close for their mix of good looks and durability. The different effects you can produce are endless, from the graphic minimalism of uniform white tiles to the unique beauty of a row of handcrafted blocks.

The current vogue on walls is for the type of heavy, expensive tile we have traditionally used on our floors, such as slate, marble, and stone. You can get them cut much thinner now, so the huge weight is no longer such a problem. And there is nothing like an expanse of delicately veined marble or sleek black slate for making a statement of real luxury—it's like having an up-scale hotel bathroom in your own home. All you need to add is an endless supply of hot water and lots of fluffy white towels. You might have to forego twenty-four hour room service though!

But in addition to these age-old tiles that are made from the earth's natural resources, there are so many up-to-the-minute products on the market—tiles that make use of the most recent technological advances. New innovations include laser cutting and cutting-edge glass technology that create the most amazing multisurface tiles that reflect light in hundreds of directions.

The hands-on element of tiling is in the selection, the creative decision-making. But when it comes to actually applying them to the walls, in most cases I would strongly advise you get an expert in. While most of us can master the basics, tiling is really a very skilled job, and I think it's a real shame when you've worked terribly hard on getting all the details exactly right to then compromise your design with a poor finish. Tiling is a very unforgiving material in this respect—shoddy work can be glaringly obvious. For smaller-scale, more rustic projects, feel free to get your hands dirty, but otherwise, get the job done professionally. To find a really good tiler, one whose workmanship will match the quality of the product you have selected to produce wonderful results, talk to tile suppliers. They can usually recommend some names.

mosaic tiles *opposite:* Visually arresting, fully water-resistant, and ideal for tiling those intricate nooks and crannies for which other tiles are just too big, mosaic is now starting to make a welcome appearance on vertical surfaces the world over.
laser-cut steel tiles *below:* Strangely, this unique idea for a room divider came about as I was experimenting with new designs for table placemats. On a whim, I had a hole drilled into the corner of each of these amazing laser-cut steel squares and then used split rings to join them together as a massive hanging curtain. The finished result, though not exactly lightweight (it needs a very solid anchor in the ceiling), is undeniably striking once in place. Position it in a room with plenty of sunlight and you will be rewarded with shadows that are a work of art in themselves.

glazed tiles *left:* It's tempting to think that the new generation of brightly colored glazed tiles now available is very avant garde. Try telling that to the Byzantine Empire of Roman Europe, where richly glazed ceramics were used to create magnificent walls of stunning proportion and effect. Well, it's only taken just over 500 years, but it looks like glazed tiles are firmly back in fashion. They are perfectly suited to splash-repelling duties, but don't be afraid to try more unconventional locations around the house.

glass tiles *opposite:* Now, these are a far more modern invention, and what a fantastic product. This particular design of glass tiles has a "two-tone" etched finish, which alters the reflected light as you change your angle of view, and so creates the impression that the whole wall is changing color as you pass. Use them near a window to maximize the effect.

working with large tiles

The ultimate in luxury bathrooms has to be fully tiled rooms; they remind me of being at some of the very best spas. Walls, floors, counters—you name it, if it's tiled, you just know it's going to look good. But just because the tiles are large, it doesn't mean the tiling is going to be easier. Far from it—the tiles are heavy and harder to handle. This really is a job for the expert, particularly if you are using anything above standard tile size. Choose your tiles wisely, but let a professional take the strain of laying.

small mosaic tile sheets

Once upon a time you needed a generous budget, and the patience of a saint, to create a large expanse of mosaic wall finish. Every single tile was adhered to the wall individually, a technique that called for a considerable amount of skill and dedication. Nowadays, you just need some ready-made sheets of tiny tiles and the talents of an amateur decorator. Widely available now in a vast range of surface finishes and colors, modern mosaics are a breeze to install and a delight to live with.

irridescent glass mosaic tiles *left:* Radically different in their designs, the practicalities of mosaic tiles remain very similar. Adhesive is applied to the walls and the sheets of tiles, already held together as handy mesh-backed panels, are pressed on in one go. These iridescent glass tiles have a truly eye-catching effect. **mosaic en masse** *opposite:* You cannot fault the timeless, understated confidence of pure white. You can even combine contrasting products to create unique designs of your own. If you don't fancy doing it yourself, there are plenty of specialists about.

tiles with textured plaster *opposite:* The most dramatic change I have witnessed to interior design over the last 20 years has been the ever-expanding range of diverse products available. There is a riot of tone and texture out there, just begging to be combined into imaginative room schemes. You may want to put those contrasting textures right up there on the wall, as I have done with this room. Stone tiles protect the splash zone, but they then give way to a wonderful textured plaster finish.
stone tiles *above:* Or you could take another design route, and contrast your walls with your furnishings. In this room wood, steel, ceramic, and fabric all jockey for your attention, but the overall effect sits quite happily and quietly in front of the powerful tranquility those stone-clad walls provide.

mosaic stone sheets

If you thought the ready-made sheets of square tiles on pages 102 and 103 were clever, wait until you try decorating with these. The principal is the same. As opposed to taking early retirement and dedicating your life to a painstaking pebble by pebble mosaicing process, these stones come ready mounted on a flexible backing and allow you to finish a wall in a weekend! The really clever part is that even though the pattern looks completely random, the individual tiling sheets are designed to tessellate together neatly for a perfect finish.

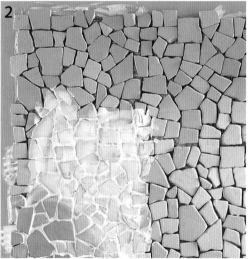

1 Working on one small area at a time (so that your adhesive doesn't harden before you can get to it), apply a layer of tile adhesive directly to the wall using a ridged plastic tile spatula. Then press the tiling sheets firmly and evenly onto the wall, interlocking the edges as you go. You can either start working across from the most obvious straight edge or, if all the surrounding surfaces are uneven, draw a perfectly aligned cross in the middle of your wall and work out from that.

2 Don't be too eager. Make sure your adhesive is completely dry before you start to grout. Be generous with the grout, and make sure you work it right down into all the cracks or air bubbles will appear as it dries. Remove the worst of the remaining surface residue with a grout scraping tool and then wipe over the surface with a wet sponge before the grout can dry. Use enough moisture to wipe the surface clean without pressing so hard with the sponge that you remove the grout from between the tiles.

opposite: I chose a white grout for this wall to show off the pattern to maximum effect. You can use grout that matches the color of the stone if you want the effect to be more subtle.

mixed ceramic tile feature wall *left:* A typical example of a mixed tile combo provides both style and protection for a bathroom splash zone with a colorful combination of sculpted tiles. Remember that embossed or textured tiles will always look more effective with oblique lighting.

hand-crafted tiles *opposite:* Tiles can also be used to frame features and make them stand out. Here I have used a vibrant combination of colors, sizes, and shapes to create a contemporary striped "barcode" feel around what would otherwise be a very plain mirror.

mixing it up with tiles

If you ask most people to close their eyes and imagine a tiled wall, chances are they are still very likely to come up with the same generic image. Square tiles. Flat tiles. Edge to edge coverage. Well, this book is here to prove that none of the above has to be true. Tiles come in all manner of shapes as well as square nowadays, more and more products have a three-dimensional or textured quality to them, and increasingly designers are using them to create feature panels on the walls of our homes.

PANELING

horizontal planks *this page:* I'm a huge fan of wooden-paneled walls and the way they work in different ways at different distances. Close up, you can see and appreciate all that lovely color and texture—take a step back and the material takes on a regular geometric quality that is umistakably wood. **woven wood** *opposite:* This unique wall paneling really does turn everything on its head. If you thought wood fencing was strictly for the backyard, this stunning bedroom will have you dragging your garden boundary indoors. Obviously a more sophisticated adaptation of familiar larch-lap panels, this room exemplifies the modern rustic theme beautifully.

PANELING

Paneling isn't a lightweight wall treatment, by any means. It adds weight and substance to a wall, both literally and in an aesthetic sense. The material you choose is the key to the look you will create. So if you want some of that loft apartment vibe, go for those industrial crossovers that are currently popular, such as rubber and glass. Or, for sheer versatility, choose wood.

It's easy to see why wood has been used to decorate our homes for centuries. We still go back to it, even with such a huge choice of alternatives available, because it has unique beauty that cannot be replicated by any other type of material. The textures and the colors are fabulous, and you can do so much with them. Look at the grain—no computer could ever come up with such an incredible design! We can enhance it with waxes and stains, colorwashes, and varnishes, but we have nature to thank for the original—we just work with what she gives us.

There's a very special feeling about using materials in your home that have been alive. Without being too hippy-trippy about it, wood has an energy. A material that has been part of the fabric of our planet can only help contribute to our global awareness, and our sense of our place in the wider world. An organic material brings a life force into our homes that a mass-produced object cannot hope to do.

Wood paneling can transform the whole feel of a space. Just as the width and direction of floorboards can completely change the perceived proportions of a room, so can wooden panels on walls. Any straight lines in a room are important because they immediately engage and lead the eye. When you have repeated lines, as with tongue-and-groove or layers of wooden boards, this effect is magnified. So when I am considering applying any form of paneling, I always take a step back and consider exactly what shape of room I'm dealing with before I make any decision about whether to go for vertical or horizontal

The texture of wood applied in different ways has a natural inherent beauty. It has an integrity of surface that comes from the fact that it was once a living material. From basic pine tongue-and-groove to oak veneer tiles, from ornate carved panels to a simply varnished masonite sheet, you can use **PANELING** to enjoy the soul and depth of wood in your home. But you can also explore more unusual materials, such as the lastest acrylic surfaces with their myriad finishes, and ultra-fashionable glass and rubber.

boards, for example. There are also the practical considerations, especially if you want to cover more than one wall in a room, such as the position of any doors and window frames, or electrical sockets and light switches.

But once you've made the basic decision, you can have some fun. Play with the shapes of the wood—uniformly cut geometric sections have a clean and graphic quality that can give a brisk, contemporary feel to a living room, for example. But I just love the way this imposed order is undercut by the random swirling patterns of the exposed wood grain (see pages 122 to 123). Some of the most beautiful woods are the hardwoods, such as cherry, walnut, and oak. They can be expensive, but if you work with the wide range of veneers that are now available, it makes the whole exercise both more practical and affordable.

To set off a kitchen or bathroom, you could use half-height tongue-and-groove paneling. This technique is a variation of the Georgian practice of applying paneling only up to the dado level in a room, so leaving the rest of the wall free to emphasize the height. Using tongue-and-groove rather than flat panels gives a fresh, almost Scandinavian feel. You can either paint the wood the same color as the rest of the walls, allowing the textures and shapes to make the statement, or give it a basic covering of wax or flat varnish to enjoy the natural finish of the wood.

Paneling has an undeniable presence, and it's important to balance this carefully in the rest of the decoration. Floor treatments, in particular, can be tricky to marry with wall paneling. Funnily enough, putting two different types of wood together successfully can be the most difficult. If you are having problems, go for a neutral flooring treatment, such as natural woven flooring.

sheet wood *opposite:* Real oak lines this wall, with a solid oak floor-to-ceiling pivoting door. You can now get large sheets of MDF that have a veneer of beautifully grained hardwood, and using these is an economical way to create an expensive-looking wall. The skill is to carefully contour the edges so they follow the vagaries of your room exactly, and to hide any mounting. **tongue-and-groove** *below:* Tongue-and-groove paneling is a quick way of covering your walls—it's probably one of the easest techniques to master for the do-it-yourself decorator.

wood tongue-and-groove *above:* If you think wooden wall finishes are strictly for the steam room, I hope I can persuade you otherwise. The natural grain of these pine planks is allowed to ghost through a subtle colorwash to show off its inherent beauty. Traditionally, tongue-and-groove paneling is used in bathroom spaces, but try thinking beyond just this to other rooms in your home.

vertical planks *opposite:* The fabulous tones of this red hardwood are allowed to shine in all their natural glory, simply accentuated with a coat of clear flat varnish. Wood will never go out of fashion, yet new ways of applying it to our walls means it will always have fresh appeal. This technique of paneling is bold and uncompromising and creates a dramatic headboard wall.

a new groove

This is a more familiar treatment, using readily available tongue-and-groove planks, only this time the slats are set in a horizontal pattern for a more contemporary effect. Here the wood is finished with a flat latex paint so the pattern of the grooves creates the characteristic look. Softwood pine is one of the most commonly cultivated trees, and as a result we see lots of it in people's homes: painting it a favorite color is our way of making it unique.

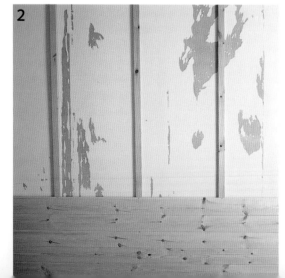

1 Tongue-and-groove is mounted on the wall using a framework of wood strips. Horizontal strips are fixed above the baseboard and below the ceiling. Then vertical strips are added every 5 feet. Light switches and sockets must be battened in the same way, as the planks need to be cut around them.

2 The slats are then nailed to the wall using the battening. Secure each slat in turn with a brad along its length at each intersection.

3 Brads are nailed through the thin "tongue" section of each plank. The "groove" of each subsequent plank laid over the top hides the nail heads, so no fixings are visible on the final wall.

opposite: The clever application of tongue-and-groove transforms a plain wall with a strong linear pattern, interesting texture, and a mass of fresh color.

contemporary wood paneling

opposite: Even the most humble of wood profiles can lift a plain and uninspiring wall. These boards, flat and as basic as they are, transcend their humble origins to create an attractive gridded framework that would enhance any room.

traditional wood paneling *right:*

Paneling lends an elegant feel to walls. This look is fairly easy to achieve with lengths of detail molding from a lumberyard, or you could use any of the ready-made paneling packs available if the thought of using a miter saw scares you. The advantage of doing it yourself, though, is that you can tailor your own panels to suit the dimensions of your room exactly.

keeping it fresh

Lots of people steer clear of paneling because they believe they will end up with a room that resembles an orange-hued sauna. But in my experience some of the most attractive homes have featured either natural pale wood or delicately painted wood paneling. Think of the beautiful wood-framed properties on New England's coast—it is the look of Martha's Vineyard or Cape Cod we are trying to emulate.

pin-stripe paneling

There are two ways you can do paneled walls—the real, expensive way, involving lots of eleborate carved wood and surly craftsmen, or the way I've done it here. This really is a very quick and easy method of making a noticeable difference to any flat expanse of wall, and with so much of variety in the style of beading strips you can buy from the hardware chains (and the infinite number of ways in which you can lay them out on the wall), there is scope for you to take on this project and really make it your own, personalizing the technique to suit your room.

1

1 Carefully measure the design of your wood bead paneling and pencil the positions onto the wall. Cut the beads to length and ideally miter the coners for a perfect joint. Run a thin line of adhesive down the back of each of the beads and then carefully nail them in place using brads and a small hammer. Make sure the nail heads end up flush with the surface of the bead so they completely disappear once everything is painted.

opposite: You'll need to vary the size of your panels to match the shape of the walls. If the room is very tall, create a design two panels high—perhaps with the bottom row slightly taller than those above.

wood panels

These panels look like solid oak but are in fact oak-veneered plywood. The effect is just the same, but the cost is an obvious saving on the real thing. Good wood merchants should have this material in stock, but you may need to order. It is worth having plenty of boards to choose from to make your final pattern, since oak grains change quite radically from one tree to the next. The lumberyard should be able to saw larger sheets down into the finished panel size you require.

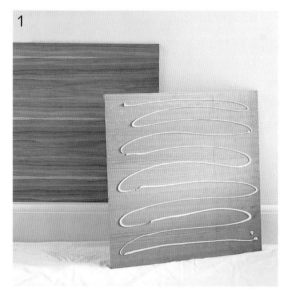

1 Apply a strong wood adhesive bonding to the reverse of each panel. Line up the panels with the straight edge of the baseboard for a true horizontal line; if there is no baseboard, position the boards on a drawn line that is perfectly straight and work from this.

2 Once the panel adhesive has dried—leave them overnight if possible— the molding can be positioned to cover any rough edges and to clean up the overall look of the panels. This curved beading strip has a simple, unfussy profile for a more contemporary effect. Glue and brad the strip in place, attaching the long vertical strips first.

3 The horizontal strips are put up last of all; simple butt joints are cut on these sections to fit closely to the vertical pieces. Glue and brad as before.

opposite: These large panels make a bold statement, but it is the undeniable beauty of the natural wood grain that makes this wall finish so eye-catching.

sparkling silver effect *left:* This silver laminate can easily replace the more traditional (dare I say ubiquitous?) stainless steel on any wall surface in the kitchen — and for a fraction of the cost and with an easier-to-look-after guarantee. Unlike steel, this surface doesn't need any painstaking baby oil treatment to keep it looking stylish.

all-over pattern *below:* This bronze covering has a quilted pattern that is immediately eye-catching. Instead of tiles against the kitchen backsplash, this finish would be both visual and durable and, unlike real copper sheets which tarnish and stain at the mere sight of a lemon squeezer, this Formica requires no aftercare.

gold-finish laminate *opposite:* I have been known to create this type of pattern on a metal sheet with the aid of a burnishing tool and a power drill. Alas, the effects were not as even as these, and the overall look not quite so pleasing. If only this material had been available then, I could have saved myself a lot of time and effort.

twenty-first century laminates

Who would have thought that much-maligned surface, good old-fashioned Formica, could look so good? The three wall treatments shown here are all examples of modern-generation Formica, so as well as looking good they are fabulously practical. This is still a great surface for kitchen walls, just for its sheer hard-wearing durability, but it is equally suited in any modern environment as an easier but just as luxurious-looking alternative to metal coverings.

glass paneling *this page:* Tiles or mosaic are the two surfaces that normally spring to mind when you are decorating a bathroom, but glass is becoming increasingly popular as an option, particularly as a single-sheet panel like this one stretched around the edge of the bathtub. **rubber** *opposite:* It's more familiar to see this material on chic loft-style apartment floors, but the owners of this London home have used it to great effect on the door fronts of this impressive bank of floor-to-ceiling closets that runs from the front of the house to the back. The push-latch fasteners on the doors make any handles redundant, so a hugely practical storage solution is cunningly disguised as a tactile and seductive wall.

grotto shells *this page:* Looking for a modern interpretation of the wonderful, eccentric, Victorian underground grottos, I created these pretty rings of tiny clam shells. The shells are glued in concentric circles around a painted composite-board base and mounted on the wall on a picture hook. Different shells create alternate looks: the black shell of a mussel, for instance, would look dramatic against a steel gray wall in a bathroom. **Moroccan rug** *opposite:* Many textiles are spoiled if left on the floor. This Moroccan rug from the Atlas Mountains is a masterpiece of woven fabric and sequins that cries out to be noticed. Against the rough pitted wall this glittering rug makes a work of art that needs no further adornment.

D I S P L A Y

In the previous sections in this book, I've talked a lot about how you can customize other people's designs, be they on wallpaper or fabric, say, to decorate your home in clever and original ways. But there is nothing to stop you from using your walls as a blank canvas for your own displays. Express yourself! You don't have to be a fine artist to create art—just use your imagination to put together an intriguing group of objects.

Antique clothing is always a great source of inspiration for me. I'm drawn to the shapes, textures, and patterns. Why hide away such gorgeous objects in darkened cupboards, I say. If you have a 1920s cocktail dress that someone once spent hours sewing hundreds of tiny sequins on, it's just a shame to neglect it. Flaunt it in all its glory, perhaps on your bedroom wall as the focal point of jazz age-inspired decoration, with lots of quilted silk bedding and some Tiffany lamps.

Rugs and other textiles are also great. Some pieces are just too precious to be trampled under foot and ignored, so highlight them by hanging them where you can see them and appreciate their beauty. Choose a wall that is hidden from the glare of natural sunlight, which can damage the delicate condition of these exquisite pieces.

Think about the type of finish of the walls you are hanging your pieces on. The undistracting bland effect of flat paint can be the best canvas for very ornate items, especially if you choose a contrasting color. You can heighten the effect of other pieces with mirror-finish polished plaster or even tightly stretched fabric.

Hanging original artwork on your walls doesn't just have to be about the content of the painting itself. Obviously one-off valuable pieces need individual treatment and a little space so they can be appreciated for what they are. But if you have a series of related prints, paintings, or photographs, you can add another aesthetic level by hanging them in an interesting way so they interact to create another design dimension (see pages 134 and 135). You can have your very own art gallery in your home, and if you want to make any changes, you can quickly dismantle your exhibition and try something new.

Exhibit a little of your own style and personality by grouping and spotlighting key elements and objects on your walls. Add some zest to your décor and reveal your style preferences and individuality by using **DISPLAY** to give your home a unique stamp. You can take the personal dynamic further by incorporating photographs of yourself, friends and family, or cherished objects that would otherwise languish in the bottom of drawers, in your displays. You can then be absolutely sure that no one else will have the same decoration as you.

As I've said many times before in this book, design is all about making pleasing patterns—the whole composition and layout, the way you like to group certain objects, what you choose to include and what you leave out, is all part of the design-making process. All these decisions reveal something about your tastes, your interests and enthusiasms. What you expose on your walls reveals something of your personality, giving your decoration an individual feel that will stand far out from the rest of the crowd.

The material can determine the effect. Hard and rigid objects, such as mirrors, can be used to make stark and graphic compositions, with well-defined shapes and outlines. More throw-away stuff can have a light-hearted appeal. Show off your *fashionista* credentials by making a collage of shopping bags from your favorite fashion stores, either applied directly to the wall using wallpaper paste and finished with a protective layer of high-gloss varnish, or captured in a set of matching picture frames with a simple profile.

I like to broaden people's imagination by playing with everyday objects. The repetitive quality of some displays can give rhythm and dynamism to a room. An ordinary object can be rendered beautiful when it is multiplied—even something as mundane as a plastic toothbrush can be made appealing. It's all down to what you do with it. If you were to display a whole wall of toothbrushes, playing with lines or blocks of color maybe, you could transform this humble bathroom tool and force people to look at it with a fresh perspective. It's your statement. It's saying that you want to have something on your walls that is out of the ordinary. Use your home to provoke comment and attention rather than letting it sink into bland uniformity.

magnetic strips *opposite:* An informal display of your life's ephemera is always fun to create, great for other people to nose through, and, let's not forget, actually very useful. The trick is to keep it fresh and topical. Magnetic strips make it easy to move things to make sure your display remains as hectic as your diary.
mirrors *below:* Mirrors are many things to many rooms—they can add space, they can add light, they can hide doors, or they can create eye-catching feature walls. Best of all, you don't need to limit your design ambitions to square or oblong shapes; most glass suppliers will now cut your mirrors to any shape you come up with. I particularly like the visual games you can play with several small mirrors clustered together. At first glance, they look like holes punched through the wall.

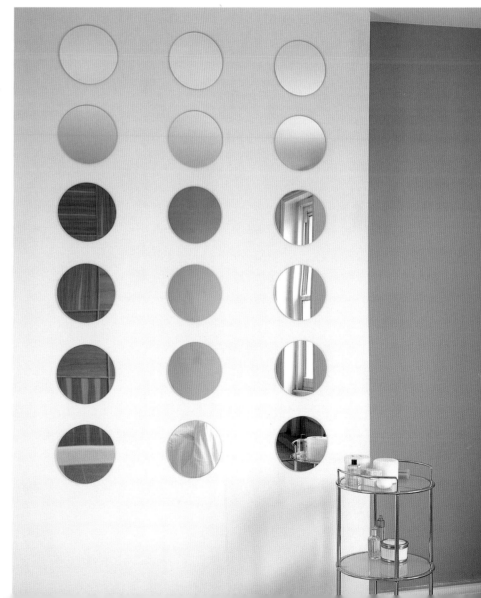

handbags *opposite:* These bags are special enough to be worth seeing on display, rather than gathering dust in the bottom of a drawer, or having only the occasional night out on your arm. It's a display that can be easily added to as your collection grows. A small nail or cup hook is all that is needed to hold the bags in place, but you could use pretty ornamental hooks for a more decorative look.

pictures *this page:* These skinny strips of wood are a feature in their own right when positioned in regular horizontal bands across a wall painted in a color that contrasts with the wood grain. Even more eye-catching then, when photos or postcards are placed along the strips. The simplicity of this display means the collection of images can be changed regularly so it will always remain fresh.

display prints on sliding doors *above:* The doors in this glamorous home
become an intrinsic part of the wall treatment. Custom made doors have a framing system
that allows the owner to exhibit chosen prints behind pieces of safety glass. When closed,
the pictures fill an entire wall. When open, the doors are manufactured in such a way that
a single panel conceals two fixed prints seamlessly, so the effect is in no way diminished.
print room *opposite:* Historically, print rooms featured images pasted on a colored wall.
Here I wanted to create the drama of a traditional print room in a fresher, more contemporary
way. These spectacular oversized prints have an incredible effect when displayed close together.

When calling the UK from the US, first dial 011 44, then drop the 0 before the number provided.

PAINT

The English Stamp Company
One of the best stamp companies with a huge range of designs
Worth Matravers
Dorset BH19 3JP, England
Tel: 01929 439117
Fax: 01929 439150
E-mail: sales@englishstamp.com
www.englishstamp.com

The Stencil Library
The world's largest mail-order stencil collection
Stocksfield Hall, Stocksfield
Northumberland NE43 7TN, England
Tel: 01661 844 844
Fax: 01661 843 984
E-mail: info@stencil-library.com
www.stencil-library.com

PaperArts
Stamping supplies such as glitter powders
Toadsmoor Road
Brimscombe, Stroud
Gloucester, GL5 2TB, England
Tel: 01453 886038
E-mail: enquiry@paperarts.co.uk
www.paperarts.co.uk

Fred Aldous Ltd
Stencils and stencil supplies such as brushes
37 Lever St
Manchester M1 1LW, England
Tel: 08707 517 300
Fax: 08707 517 303
E-mail: Aldous@btinternet .com
www.fredaldous.co.uk

Henny Donovan Motif
Unique high-quality designer stencils and metallic stencil paints
10 Brook Lodge
Coolhurst Road
London N8 8ER, England
Tel: 020 8340 0259
E-mail: salesinfo@hennydonovanmotif.co.uk
www.hennydonovanmotif.co.uk

Artboxdirect
Artists' materials from manufacturers such as Daler-Rowney and Winsor & Newton
23/25 The Pollet
St Peter Port
Guernsey GY1 1WQ, England
Tel : 01481 701351
Fax: 01481 710383
E-mail: info@artboxdirect.com
www.artboxdirect.co.uk

Daler-Rowney
High quality artists' materials, including paints and brushes
PO Box 10
Bracknell RG12 8ST, England
Tel: 01344 461000
Fax: 01344 486511
E-mail: customer.service@daler-rowney.com
www.daler-rowney.com

Benjamin Moore & Co
A wide range of paints and home decorating products. Stores located throughout the U.S. and Canada.
www.benjaminmoore.com

Belvedere Books, Inc.
Copyright-free images
International Publications
P. O. Box 12.301
I - 00135 Rome, Italy
Tel: +39 06 3550 5531
Fax: +39 06 3550 5555
E-mail : info@belvedere-books.com
www.belvedere-books.com

Crown Paints
Extensive range of colors and types, including suede-effect emulsion
P.O. Box 37
Crown House
Hollins Road, Darwen
Lancashire BB3 0BG, England
Tel: 0870 240 1127
E-mail: http://www.crownpaint.co.uk/contact/
www.crownpaint.co.uk

Craig & Rose Paints
A range of paints, including glitter, glaze, and metallic
Unit 8
Halbeath Industrial Estate
Crossgates Road
Dunfermline
Fife KY11 7EG, Scotland
Tel: 01383 740 011
E-mail: enquiries@craigandrose.com
www.craigandrose.com

Farrow & Ball Ltd
Traditional paint manufactured to original formulations
Uddens Estate
Wimborne
Dorset BH21 7NL, England
Tel: 01202 876141
Fax: 01202 873793
E-mail: info@farrow-ball.com
www.farrow-ball.com

Fired Earth
Rich paint colors inspired by international styles
3 Twyford Mill
Oxford Road
Adderbury
Near Banbury
Oxfordshire OX17 3SX, England
Tel: 01295 812088
Fax: 01295 810832
E-mail: enquiries@firedearth.com
www.firedearth.com

The Little Greene Paint Company Ltd
A wide range of paints, including the Catwalk collection that reflects the latest fashion colors
Wood Street
Openshaw
Manchester M11 2FB, England
Tel: 0161 230 0880
Fax: 0161 223 3208
E-mail: mail@thelittlegreene.com
www.thelittlegreene.com

The Paint & Paper Library
Inspirational paints with a unique vitality and depth of color
18 Pond Place
London SW3 6QJ, England
Tel: 020 7823 7755
Fax: 020 7823 7766
E-mail: info@paintlibrary.co.uk
www.paintlibrary.co.uk

Zoffany
Rich colors in flat latex, eggshell, and gloss
Chalfont House
Oxford Road, Denham
Uxbridge UB9 4DX, England
Tel: 08708 300 350
Fax: 08708 300 352
Email: enquiries@zoffany.uk.com
www.zoffany.co.uk

APPLICATIONS

HobbyCraft Group Ltd
Mail-order craft supplies, including gilding materials
7 Enterprise Way
Aviation Park
Bournemouth International Airport
Christchurch
Dorset BH23 6HG, England
Tel: 0800 027 2387
Fax: 01202 596101
www.hobbycraft.co.uk

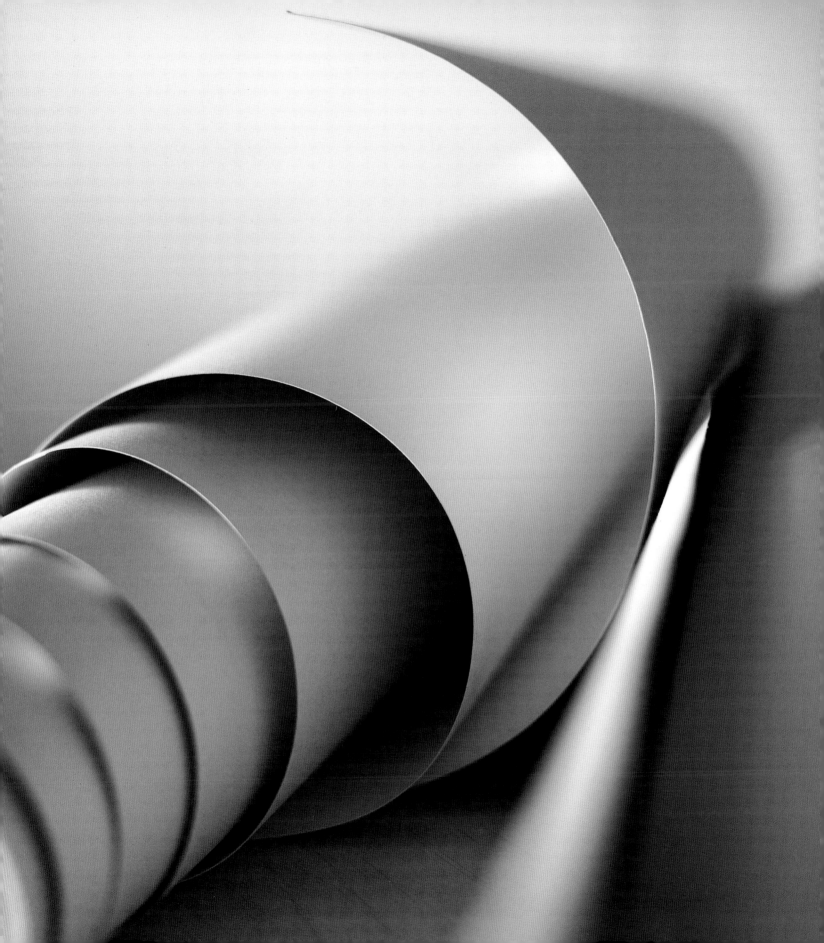

Scribblers
Gilding sheets, glues, and bronzing powders
12 Witney Road
Pakefield, Lowestoft
Suffolk NR33 7AW, England
Tel: 01502 562392
E-mail: mail@scribblers.co.uk
www.scribblers.co.uk

Armourcoat Surface Finishes
Decorative wall finishes
4629 South 136th Street
Omaha, NE 68137, USA
Tel: 402-896-2005
Toll Free: 888-368-5893
Fax: 402-895-7238
E-mail: sales@armourcoatusa.com
www.armourcoatusa.com

Calfe Crimmings
Handcrafted polished plaster finishes
6 Nylands Avenue
Kew, Surrey TW9 4HH, England
Tel: 0208 847 1561
Fax: 0208 876 1773
E-mail: enquiry@calfecrimmings.co.uk
www.calfecrimmings.co.uk

The Polished Plaster Company
Italian plaster in a variety of finishes and colors
Tel: 01535 646866
Fax: 0870 7623738
E-mail: info@polishedplaster.co.uk
www.polishedplaster.co.uk

Swarovski Crystal
Wall tattoos
1 Kenney Drive
Cranston, RI 02920-4468, USA
Tel: 800-426-3088
Fax: 800-870-5660
E-mail: customer_relations.gb@swarovski.com
www.shop.swarovski.com

Really Linda Barker Limited
Mail-order home furnishings and decorative accessories
PO Box 24929
Forest Hill, London SE23 3WU, England
Tel: 0870 242 0651
www.reallylindabarker.co.uk

The Stencil Library
Paint stencils of all sizes and designs
see PAINT

Ceramic Decals Ltd
Wall transfers/tattoos
Anderton Works
Port Street, Middleport
Stoke-on-Trent
Staffordshire ST6 3PF, England
Tel: 0178283 8000
E-mail: reception@ceramicdecals.co.uk
www.ceramicdecals.co.uk

Dover Publications, Inc.
Copyright-free images
Customer Care Department
31 East 2nd Street
Mineola, NY 11501-3852, USA
Fax: 516-742-6953
www.store.doverpublications.com

WALLPAPER

Deborah Bowness
Wallpaper designer
401.5 Workshops
Wandsworth Road
London SW8 2JP, England
Tel: 07817 807 504
E-mail: info@deborahbowness.com
www.deborahbowness.com

Graham & Brown Wallpapers
A range of designs, including natural grasscloths
P.O. Box 39
India Mill, Harwood Street
Blackburn, Lancashire BB1 3DB, England
Tel: 01254 691 321
Email: help.is@grahambrown.com
www.grahambrown.com

Myfotowall Ltd
Custom-made photographic wallpaper
90 New North Road, Huddersfield
West Yorkshire HD1 5NE, England
Tel: 01484 344 096
E-mail: customer-services@myfotowall.com
www.myfotowall.com

Louise Body Wallprint
Hand-finished contemporary wallpaper
Tel: 01273 711601
E-mail: louise@louisebodywallprint.com
www.louisebodywallprint.com

Cole & Son Wallpapers
Traditional wallpaper manufacturers
Lee Jofa Inc.
201 Central Avenue South
Bethpage, NY 11714, USA
Tel: 516-752-7600
E-mail: customer.service@cole-and-son.com
www.cole-and-son.com

de Gournay Wallpapers
Hand-painted wallpapers, specialists in Chinoiserie
112 Old Church Street, Chelsea
London SW3 6EP, England
Tel: 020 7823 7316
Fax: 020 7823 7475
E-mail: info@degournay.com
www2.degournay.com

Osborne & Little
Fantastic modern florals
304 King's Road
London SW3 5UH, England
Tel: 020 7352 1456
Fax: 020 7351 7813
E-mail: showroom@osborneandlittle.com
www.osborneandlittle.com

Interactive Wallpaper
Custom-made and limited edition wallpaper designed by Rachel Kelly
Tel: 020 7490 3076
E-mail: studio@interactivewallpaper.co.uk
www.interactivewallpaper.co.uk

Cabbages & Roses
Pretty floral wallpapers
3 Langton Street
London SW10 0JL, England
Tel: 020 7352 7333
Fax: 020 7351 3666
E-mail: enquiries@cabbagesandroses.com
www.cabbagesandroses.com

Farrow & Ball Ltd
Still manufacture using traditional methods.
see PAINT

Cath Kidston
Signature floral prints with a retro feel
Designers Guild
3 Latimer Place, London W10 6QT, England
Tel: 020 7893 7700
Fax: 020 7893 7720
E-mail: info@designersguild.com
www.cathkidston.co.uk

Designers Guild
Vibrant modern designs
3 Latimer Place, London W10 6QT, England
Tel: 020 7893 7400
Fax: 020 7893 7720
E-mail: info@designersguild.com
www.designersguild.com

CWV Ltd
A range of wallpapers, including Coloroll, Vymura, Jeff Banks and Benetton
Number One@The Beehive
Shadsworth Business Park
Lions Drive, Blackburn
Lancashire BB1 2QS, England
Tel: 01254 222800
www.wallpapers-uk.com

Zoffany
Rich, traditional designs that look at home even in contemporary interiors
Chalfont House
Oxford Road, Denham
Uxbridge UB9 4DX, England
Tel: 08708 300 350
Fax: 08708 300 352
E-mail: enquiries@zoffany.uk.com
www.zoffany.co.uk

The Natural Floor Company
Flooring materials that can be applied to the wall
389 King Street
London W6 9NJ, England
Tel: 020 8741 4451
E-mail: sales@thenaturalfloorcompany.com
www.thenaturalfloorcompany.com

Neisha Crosland
Wrapping papers, wallpaper, and fabric
8 Elystan Street
London SW3 3NS, England
Tel: 020 7584 7988
Fax: 020 7584 7999
Tel: 020 7978 4389
E-mail: elystanstreet@neishacrosland.com
www.neishacrosland.com

Marian Cotterill Wallpapers
*Vintage wallpapers, including
Florence Broadhurst designs*
Lounge (London) Ltd
Ms Marian Cotterill
6 Mapesbury Road
London NW2 4HY, England
Tel: 020 8931 6649
Fax: 020 8451 0895
E-mail: mariancotterill@btinternet.com
www.loungeonline.net

The Stencil Library
The world's largest mail-order stencil collection
see PAINT

FABRIC

Wilman Interiors
*Printed and woven fabrics, from contemporary
to classic.*
CWV Group Ltd
Heasandford Industrial Estate
Widow Hill Road
Burnley
Lancashire BB10 2TJ, England
E-mail: wilman.enquiries@cwvgroup.com
www.wilman.co.uk

Screen Productions Ltd
*Ready-made and custom photographic
print products*
176 Hydethorpe Road
London SW12 0JD, England
Tel: 020 8675 9735
E-mail: claire.holmes@screenproductions.co.uk
www.screenproductions.co.uk

Alma Leather
Wall coverings in suede and leather
8 Vigo Street
London W15 3HJ, England
Tel: 020 7377 0762
Fax: 020 7375 2471
E-mail: info@almahome.co.uk
www.almahome.co.uk

Bill Amberg
Custom-made leather wall treatments
The Workshops
31 Elkstone Road
London W10 5NT, England
Tel: 020 8960 2000
Fax: 020 8960 2321
www.billamberg.com

Monkwell Fabrics
An extensive range of textiles
227 Kings Road
London SW3 5EJ, England
Tel: 01825 747 903
Fax: 01825 761397
E-mail: enquiries@monkwell.com
www.monkwell.com

Emma Jeffs
Wall coverings, including lace laminates
Surfacematerialdesign
17 Skiffington Close
London SW2 3UL, England
Tel: 020 8671 3383
Fax: 020 8671 3383
E-mail: info@surfacematerialdesign.co.uk
www.surfacematerialdesign.co.uk

Crowson Fabrics
A fabric supplier with a large range
Crowson House, Bellbrook Park
Uckfield
East Sussex TN22 1QZ, England
Tel: 01825 761055
Fax: 01825 764 517
E-mail: sales@crowsonfabrics.com
www.crowsonfabrics.com

Muraspec
Commercial wall coverings
74–8 Wood Lane End
Hemel Hempstead
Hertfordshire HP2 4RF, England
Tel: 08705 117 118
Fax: 08705 329 020
E-mail: customerservices@muraspec.com
www.muraspec.com

Cath Kidston
Signature floral prints with a retro feel
see WALLPAPER

Designers Guild
*Vibrant modern designs with a great selection of
colors and patterns*
see WALLPAPER

Zoffany
*Rich, traditional designs that look at home even in
contemporary interiors*
see WALLPAPER

Neisha Crosland
Wrapping papers, wallpaper, and fabric
see WALLPAPER

Beautiful Saris
UK-based website selling a huge range of sari cloths
E-mail: cbm@beautifulsaris.co.uk
www.beautifulsaris.co.uk

The Cotton Patch
Natural and man-made fabrics
1285 Stratford Road
Hall Green
Birmingham B28 9AJ, England
Tel: 0121 702 2840
Fax: 0121 778 5924
E-mail: mailorder@cottonpatch.net
www.cottonpatch.co.uk

Queenshill
*On-line mail-order company who sells fabrics by
Malabar, Sanderson, Lee Jofa and Jewel*
South Lodge, Queens Hill
Ascot
Berkshire SL5 7EG, England
Tel: 01344 875419
E-mail: service@queenshill.com
www.queenshill.com

TILING

Jali Home Design
Individually made screens and fretwork panels
Albion Works, Church Lane
Barham, Canterbury
Kent CT4 6QS, England
Tel: 01227 833333
Fax: 01227 831950
www.jali.co.uk

Reed Harris Tiles
Tiling and bathroom supplies
Riverside House
27 Carnwath Road
London SW6 3HR, England
Tel: 020 8877 9774
www.reedharris.co.uk

Island Stone
Floor and wall coverings
78 York Street
London W1H 1DP, England
Tel: 0800 083 9351
E-mail: sales@islandstone.co.uk
www.islandstone.co.uk

Fired Earth
A selection of beautiful hand-crafted tiles
see PAINT

The Stone & Ceramic Warehouse
Imported Italian and Spanish products
51/55 Stirling Road
London W3 8DJ, England
Tel: 020 8993 5545
Fax: 020 8752 0281
E-mail: gen@stoneandceramicwarehouse.co.uk
www.stoneandceramicwarehouse.co.uk

Porcelanosa
Spanish company with showrooms all over the US
Tel: 877-767-7287
www.porcelanosa-usa.com

Stonehouse Tiles
Suppliers of stone, limestone, marble, and granite
42 Enterprise Business Estate
Bolina Road, London SE16 3LF, England
Tel: 0800 0939 724
E-mail: info@stonehousetiles.co.uk
www.stonehousetiles.co.uk

CLADDING

Rummages
Reclaimed timber and custom joinery
Hieraticha Works, Unit 9
12 Argall Avanue, London E10 7QE, England
Tel: 020 8539 9333
E-mail: info@rummages4wood.com
www.rummages4wood.com

Timber to Go
Suppliers of all types of timber
255 Lythalls Lane, Coventry CV6 6FW, England
Tel: 024 76 688 886
E-mail: sales@timbertogo.com
www.timbertogo.com

Alsford Timber
Timber, sheet materials, and joinery
Junction of Oakfield Lane and Lowfield Street
Dartford, Kent DA1 2SN, England
Tel: 01322 333088
Fax: 01322 289510
E-mail: dartford@alsfordtimber.com
www.alsfordtimber.com

Formica Ltd
Decorative laminates
255 East 5th Street
Suite 200
Cincinnati, OH 45202, USA
Tel: 1-800-FORMICA
www.formica.com

Pearsons Glass Ltd
All types of glass cut and drilled to specific needs
Maddrell Street
Liverpool L3 7EH, England
Tel: 0151 207 1474
Fax: 0151 207 4039
Email: marketing@pearsonsglass.co.uk
www.pearsonsglass.com

Dalsouple
Rubber for floors and walls
P.O. Box 140, Bridgwater
Somerset TA5 1HT, England
Tel: 01278 727 733
Fax: 01278 727 766
E-mail: info@dalsouple.com
www.dalsouple.com

The Rubber Flooring Company
Sheet and tile flooring that can also be applied to walls
Unit 12, Smallshaw Industrial Estate
Burnley, Lancashire BB11 5SX, England
Tel: 01282 411014
Fax: 01282 411015
E-mail: mail@trfco.co.uk
www.the rubberflooringcompany.co.uk

DISPLAY

Hilary Proctor Antique Handbags
A great source of beautiful objects
1–7 Davis Mews, London W1, England
Tel: 07956 876428
E-mail: hproctor@antiquehandbags.fsnet.co.uk

Trowbridge Prints
Framed prints and pictures
555 Kings Road
London, SW6 2EB, England
Tel: 0870 403 0005
Fax: 0870 403 0410
E-mail: gallery@trowbridge.co.uk
www.trowbridgegallery.com

Ikea Furnishings
Furniture, accessories, shelving, mirrors and picture frames
www.ikea.com

Pearsons Glass Ltd
Mirror and decorative glass cut to size
see CLADDING

Mirror Mirror
All types and styles of mirrors
133 Dean Road, Scarborough
North Yorkshire YO12 7JH, England
Tel: 01723 350050
Fax: 01723 370022
E-mail: info@mirror-mirror.com
www.mirror-mirror.com

Alsford Timber
Timber, sheet materials and joinery
see CLADDING

Frame-Express Picture Framers Ltd
Frames made to order
57 Barkers Butts Lane
Coundon
Coventry CV6 1DU, England
Tel: 024 7659 3529
E-mail: sales@frame-express.net
www.frame-express.net

Fast Frames
On-line company making frames to order
Tel: 0871 550 0031
Fax: 0870 855 5408
E-mail: info@fastframes.co.uk
www.fastframes.co.uk

C. Best
Homewares
Units P50–55, New Covent Garden Flower Market
Vauxhall, London SW8 5NA, England
Tel: 020 7720 2306

ACCESSORIES

Hampstead Garden Centre
Pots, urns, and decorative accessories
163 Iverson Road
London NW6 2HH, England
Tel: 020 7328 3208

Laura Ashley Ltd
Furniture and decorative accessories
US Headquarters
7000 Regent Parkway
Fort Mill, SC 29715, USA
Tel: 803-396-7744
E.mail: customerservice@lauraashley-usa.com
www.lauraashley.com

Really Linda Barker Ltd
Furniture and decorative accessories
see APPLICATIONS

Roca Ltd
Bathroom Accessories
Samson Road
Hermitage Industrial Estate
Coalville
Leicestershire LE67 3FP, England
Tel: 01530 830 080
E-mail: sales@roca-uk.com
www.roca-uk.com

Edmund de Waal
Ceramics
E-mail: studio@edmunddewaal.com
www.edmunddewaal.com

Jill Ford Ceramics
Ceramic vases and wall plaques
Providence House
Main Street
Ellerton
East Riding of Yorks YO42 4PB, England
E-mail: Jillfordceramics@aol.com
www.jillford.com

Mrs Robinson
Home furnishings and accessories
128/130 Lordship Lane
London SE22 8HD, England
Tel: 020 8693 0693

Anne Middleton
Ceramic Vases
Arch 191
Blenheim Court, Blenheim Grove
London SE15, England
Tel: 020 7639 1550

INDEX

ACKNOWLEDGMENTS

There is an inescapable hierarchy when doing this acknowledgment thing, and I should start right up there with the top billing. It's been fabulous to work on a book again, after a long break of several years during which I was always being told "the market just isn't ready for another interior book right now" or, if it was ready, I was always too busy to do anything about it! Finally, it seems the market and my diary are in agreement, and I do genuinely want to thank my British publisher Jacqui Small for offering me this opportunity to get back to work on a prestige publishing project. As ever, my agent Fiona Lindsay was also instrumental in the deal and, among the many things I still need to thank her for, I must now include getting Jacqui and me together. Jacqui produces fabulous books and I feel privileged to be working as one of her authors—a very coveted position in my line of work.

The book dedication, you may have noticed, is to my good friends Lou and Brian. Brian post-produced all the images, while Lou is the photographer of this lovely book—I'm sure you have thoroughly enjoyed her wonderful shots. Over the years Lou and I have worked on a number of projects and I always love her work, her enthusiasm and her humor—which is pretty infectious, but only to those of us who have been working the same long hours. . . It's a great thing when you are fortunate enough to look forward to going to work, even on a Monday morning, and I have had that feeling ever since we started shooting this book. I thank Lou for that.

Now, it would be all the more impressive if I said the book was a terrible struggle, that I battled with the text until midnight for weeks on end, that we shot the photographs over long arduous months, but sadly I can't, because none of that is true and on the whole the entire thing was an absolute joy. I love working on shoots like ours, I love the creative process, I love to pull the shots together and work as part of a small team to get things done. My small team in particular always deserves special acknowledgement, so great thanks go to Helen for organizing our days, Nick for the decorating, Simon for the more specialized wall finishes, and particularly Cesca, Lou's small but perfectly formed assistant. It's amazing someone can play so large a part in the shoot, and yet take up so little room in the studio.

Thanks too for Brian, Lou's husband, who got all the pictures ready to print. Somehow, that job sounds too easy, doesn't it? Brian, I know it's not—you even ironed out some of my creases with Photoshop (without me even having to ask) so I'm grateful for the few extra years you've given me! Also, warm thanks to the publishing team, Kate John for getting us all to start (and getting us all to finish) Sian Parkhouse, who helped me with getting the words onto paper, and, of course, Valerie Fong, for making sure that whatever did end up on paper landed in exactly the right place—you did a beautiful job designing the layout.

My greatest thanks though are to my husband. Chris and I have been together for a long old time. He knew me when I was a struggling, teenage art student—without a dime, let alone a career. We've grown up together if you like, and I think we're still doing just that. He's endured the highs and lows of my checkered career, and after more than 20 years is still here—sometimes that seems like a miracle. After "I'm a Celebrity, Get Me Out Of Here" the press gave us six months! How little these people really know about other people's lives. He is my everything. (Now where's that pre-nuptial agreement?)

And finally, the one person who makes it all worthwhile, Jessica. Sorry about your bedroom, darling.